Counseling Theories

Edited by

Clyde A. Parker

University of Minnesota

and Counselor Education

Houghton Mifflin Company
Boston

New York
Atlanta
Geneva, Illinois
Dallas
Palo Alto

Foreword

The professional education of counselors in the United States is a lively but uncoordinated movement. I started to write that counselor education is "a messy affair" but that would be most unjust to a score or two of universities in which there are carefully designed graduate programs. These are soundly based on psychological understandings and contain reasonably substantial provisions for competency in psychological measurement. A good bit of attention is given to an understanding of the counseling process. There is a growing tendency for a block of time in the curriculum to be devoted to supervised counseling experience with individuals and with groups. These "better" programs provide a careful balance between mastery of ideas and experience with people, between knowing and doing.

The critical observer of counselor education in American universities has much to say, however, about the pedantic emphasis upon abstract principles and organizational outlines on the one hand and quickly outdated information and techniques on the other hand. Many programs are jerry-built and opportunistic. Until the 1960's, no professional organization in the field established criteria or standards for the first graduate year of counselor education—the Division of Counseling Psychology of the American Psychological Association proposed standards at the doctorate level in 1952. Following the report of the Commission on Guidance in American Schools in 1962 (*The Counselor in a Changing World*), the American Personnel and Guidance Association and two of its Divisions established criteria for counselor performance and counselor education. There is as yet, however, no national body which evaluates or certifies programs of study. As a consequence, there is a very uneven and unstable quality of preparation offered throughout the country.

Even more apparent is the failure of most programs to be clearly related to any organized psychological theory or philosophical value system. It is at this point that the present book makes a distinct contribution. Dr. Parker, a one-time teaching assistant of mine and now at the University of Minnesota, makes its possible for the reader to examine four distinct personality approaches and the manner in which they are believed to affect a counselor education program. The rejoinders to each of the four major papers were made by men who believed differently—and deeply so—but who evidenced the greatest respect for the paper being criticized. These four views are examined in some depth, both pro and con, and the differences are as apparent as is the line-up in a garden of rows of carrots, tomatoes, onions, and squash.

To me this book is lively reading. The rebuttals are as fresh and creative as are the papers to which they are a response. The openness of the "Encounter" between the members of the seminar following each pair of papers is very human—and very readable. Dr. Parker's first-chapter analysis of the issues facing counselors and counselor education is in itself worth the price of admission. The participating members of the seminar represent the best in "young" thinking about human behavior; they interact with vigor and good comradeship. The book as a whole throws a shaft of rather intense light upon the current psychological foundations of counseling in America.

C. Gilbert Wrenn

Preface

Professional counseling is still a relatively new institution in our society, and some critics continue to doubt the uniform effectiveness of counseling. However, it does seem clear that a counselor is able to effect changes in a client's behavior, attitudes, and emotions—changes that should signal improvement in the client's condition but may sometimes indicate a deterioration. Recognition of the possibility of negative effects places a heavy burden on counselor educators who have the responsibility of certifying a counselor's competence. At present, there is little theory or research to guide the educator in developing curriculum or supervisory procedures.

The University of Minnesota Counselor Education Seminar was held specifically to enlist counselor educators of the Upper Midwest region in the examination of a developing theory of counselor education. The Seminar was held May 14–17, 1967, at Izaty's Lodge in Onamia, Minnesota. Representatives from eleven institutions which prepare professional counselors in the five-state region (North Dakota, South Dakota, Minnesota, Iowa, and Wisconsin) were invited. Approximately 45 persons attended.

The structure of the seminar allowed almost continuous dialogue between those who prepared and presented papers and those who "attended" so that one can quite properly refer to all present as "participants." Four pairs of papers were prepared and distributed in advance: the first paper of a pair was a statement on a controversial issue, the second was a rebuttal. After each pair, there was a discussion period in which participants freely expressed their own views. Certainly the success of the seminar was dependent upon the intense and provocative conversations that resulted. This format facilitated the critical evaluation of ideas.

This text contains the prepared papers and excerpts from the discussions that followed each pair of papers. It also contains my own introductory chapter which clarifies the needs in counselor

education and poses the questions which prompted the organization of the Seminar. Counselor educators and others whose primary concern is the preparation of clinical personnel are the
audience to which the papers were addressed and should find
them especially helpful. Since each paper initially established the
counseling premises upon which the preparation programs were
based, counselors and clinicians in preparation will find the content valuable. Finally, because the approaches taken in the papers
deviate from typical personality models, practitioners interested
in a fresh look at their approach will find a new perspective in
one or more of the papers.

The immediate result of the Seminar has been the development of a new sequence in the curriculum of the Minnesota
program which combines the basic counseling theory course with
the practicum and integrates the experiential, cognitive, and
clinical approaches which are presented in detail in the Gibb,
Levy, Vance, and Blocher papers. The subsequent feedback
which the Minnesota staff has received from the other participants has sharpened our views and our approach. We are in-
debted to these participants for their contributions.

I would like to express appreciation to Dean Keller of the
College of Education of the University of Minnesota, who made
available the funds for the seminar; and to the faculty of the
Counselor Education department, Drs. Alan R. Anderson, Donald H. Blocher, Wesley W. Tennyson, and Lyle D. Schmidt,
who helped directly in the planning and execution of the seminar; and most especially to those who contributed the papers,
Drs. Donald H. Blocher, Edward Bordin, Jack R. Gibb, Leon H.
Levy, C. H. Patterson, Harold B. Pepinsky, Charles B. Truax,
and Forrest L. Vance. Finally my thanks to those many persons
not named whose interest, support, and encouragement led us to
go ahead with the project.

Clyde A. Parker

Contents

The Contributors

Donald H. Blocher, Professor of Educational Psychology, has taught at the University of Minnesota since 1960. He completed his Ph.D. at the University of Minnesota in 1959. He is the author of numerous papers on counseling theory and philosophy and his recent text *Developmental Counseling* has been widely used. He is currently doing research on counselor preparation.

Edward Bordin is Chief of Counseling in the Bureau of Psychological Services and Professor of Psychology at the University of Michigan. He is the author of *Psychological Counseling*. His research and writing interests have taken him into adolescent development, and the development of vocational interests as well as counseling and psychotherapy. A 1942 Ph.D. from Ohio State University, he is well known for his diverse and extensive contributions to counseling psychology.

Jack R. Gibb is somewhat of a maverick in the field of counseling. His area of special interest is organizational development and his preparation and research is in the area of small groups. A 1943 Stanford University Ph.D., he taught at several universities, helped establish the N.T.L. training laboratories, and engaged in private consulting before becoming a fellow at The Western Behavioral Science Institute where he was affiliated at the time of the Seminar. Since then he has returned to private practice. He is the co-author of *T-Group Theory and Laboratory Method* in addition to his many papers on small groups and organizational development.

Leon H. Levy, Professor of Psychology at Indiana University, is the author of *Psychological Interpretation*. He obtained his Ph.D. from Ohio State University in 1954. Since then he has maintained an interest in personality theory which is reflected in his published papers.

C. H. Patterson is Professor of Educational Psychology and Chairman of the Division of Counselor Education at the University of Illinois. A University of Minnesota Ph.D. of 1955, and a prolific writer, his published works include *Theories of Counseling and Psychotherapy* and *Counseling and Guidance in Schools*.

Harold B. Pepinsky is a University of Minnesota Ph.D (1946) now Professor of Psychology and of Computer and Information Science at the Ohio State University. Combining substantive interests from the two fields, his research centers on human information production exchange and use—ranging in scope from the study of institutionalized help-giving to the two-person encounter as exemplified by counseling and negotiation. His numerous theoretical and research publications in counseling psychology are exemplified by his text (with Pauline N. Pepinsky) *Counseling: theory and practice*.

Charles B. Truax, Director of Research in the Arkansas Rehabilitation Research and Training Center and Professor of Psychology at the University of Arkansas, is engaged in extensive research to identify relevant variables in the counseling process. His recent text (with Robert Carkhuff) *Toward an Effective Counseling and Psychotherapy: Training and Practice* is an excellent review of current and existing research with implications for both the counseling process and preparation programs.

Forrest L. Vance is Director of the University Counseling Center and Professor of Counseling and Psychology at the University of Rochester. A 1958 University of Minnesota Ph.D. he has continued the clinical practice of counseling and psychotherapy with the exception of a brief period when he was an administrative officer for the American Psychological Association. The philosophy of science is among his many interests and through his published papers he has helped the profession focus on some of our difficult philosophical problems.

Counseling Theories
and Counselor Education

1

Issues, Evidence, and a Beginning

CLYDE A. PARKER
University of Minnesota

"Counseling is serious business. Across a counselor's desk come the aspirations and anxieties, the convictions and the difficult choices that have generated all the theories about human personality" (Tyler, 1958).

In this short statement Tyler encapsulated the perplexing problems which have faced the counseling profession. Because of the intended intervention in another person's life, the behavior of a counselor *is* serious business—and the concern of his many publics as well as of the client. In the schools, the principal, faculty, and supporting staff all feel the counselor's effectiveness or lack of it. Parents are rightfully concerned with the ultimate influence of the counselor's action on their child. With the extensive involvement of counselors in the Great Society programs and the widespread acceptance of the mental health movement, the impact of counseling has become a serious matter to many more people. We long have recognized that the attempt to intervene in another person's life is not inconsequential. The striking fact of today is the general approval of counseling in our society, often without critical examination of its appropriateness to the activity at hand.

The greater significance of Tyler's comment is in her recognition of the diversity of problems with which counselors have been faced and the possible relation of this diversity to the many theories that have been generated to explain and to cope with man's behavior. The helping professions have developed literally dozens of "approaches." An "approach" derives principally from a person who has had singular success with a particular popula-

1

tion of clients or selected range of problems. His personal effectiveness has been systematized and often generalized to the full range of human concerns. Almost immediately a cadre of followers for whom the methods "fit" jump on the bandwagon and go "full steam ahead." One of the more recent of these is Glasser's (1965) *Reality Therapy*, developed primarily with delinquent girls but broadened, by Glasser, to include outpatient neurotics, hospitalized psychotics, and college students. Professionals who have been looking for a rationale for their more aggressive intervention modes have quickly joined the movement with little or no systematic investigation of the effectiveness of their methods. The profession might be better characterized by its rapid "theory seizures" than by its hard evidence of value. Unfortunately, the original effectiveness of the leader is seldom transmitted to his followers. The messianic hopes dwindle as the disciples imitate their leader without possessing the spirit that inspired him. This situation has posed many problems for various "schools" of counseling or therapy.

The profession has always been sharply divided between polarities, as in the directive-nondirective controversy of twenty years ago, or the behaviorism-existentialism debates now current. Our reliance upon philosophical and theoretical "positions" rather than effectiveness of selected interventions may reflect as much about the persons attracted to the profession as it does about the state of our knowledge. "Compassion" rather than "doubt" is the characteristic description (Bordin, 1966). Explanations that promise to guide action are readily bought and often tenaciously held without the systematic examination characteristic of an experimental psychologist. In between such debates there have been attempts to identify the common elements (Rogers, 1957), to systematically relate different theories (Ford and Urban, 1963), or to develop an integrated eclecticism (Brammer and Shostrum, 1960). To date there is little evidence that a comprehensive system will soon emerge that will provide adequate preparation for a single person to cope with all of the situations with which he could be asked for help.

Under these circumstances, is there any clear direction for counselor educators? With the proliferation of counseling theories, the counselor educator has the onerous task of fashioning some systematic program of experiences out of which will emerge a competent professional. We have done little theorizing about what those experiences should be and even less investigating of our results to date.

The seminar reported in this volume was organized with the underlying belief that the profession had reached a point developmentally where it needed to turn upon itself and begin to consider more intensively *the process by which a counselor becomes effective.* This is not the first extended meeting with such an agenda. Both clinical psychology and counseling psychology have, from time to time, attempted to specify the ingredients of training programs. But this seminar was initiated from a different and, we hope, more productive base. We (1) started with some theoretical constructs of the effective counselor, (2) abstracted from these general counselor behaviors, and then (3) asked persons readily identified with particular "schools" to construct model education programs to maximize the likelihood of a counselor's being effective.

Inherent in most systematic approaches to counseling are some implicit injunctions about how counselors ought to be prepared. Because of the expected interference of repressed material in the analyst's effectiveness, Freud and his followers insisted that an analyst be analyzed. Convinced that the relationship was the effective ingredient, Rogers made early claims that psychological content was unnecessary and that he could prepare counselors adequately in a few weeks. D. G. Paterson, on the other hand, never was interested in preparing counselors per se but wanted to develop differential psychologists. The fact that a number of his students have become well-known counselors or counselor educators was somewhat incidental to his interest. For many, however, becoming an adequate counselor has involved an unspecified mixture of mastering the conceptual scheme or schemes and undergoing supervised experience.

With the advent of counseling psychology and later the development of school counseling under the aegis of the NDEA, various professional bodies have developed lists of courses or specified content necessary for the stamp of approval of the respective professional groups. The plurality of theoretical positions represented in those bodies has resulted more in conglomerates of generalities than in programs based on any systematic theory that can be tested and then related to effective counseling. A professional counselor, then, is by definition one who has completed a "professional" course. From one standpoint this concept has been necessary and desirable to ensure the unfettered development of a young profession. From another it has allowed an uncontrolled proliferation of programs that have escaped evaluation.

Issues in Counselor Preparation

The lack of evaluation is no doubt due to several factors besides the absence of a substantive theory to guide the program. One factor is the pressure to produce counselors to fill existing vacancies. Another is the lack of research funds for evaluation. (Who ever really asks appraisal questions of higher education?) Resistance comes too from the threat involved in learning about one's ineffectiveness and the sheer complexity of relating effective teaching to effective counseling. Several issues have been presented throughout this professional growth process. We have had little with which to resolve them except our personal convictions and prejudices about what good counseling is or how a good counselor behaves. As a basis for understanding the rationale of the papers which follow, let us examine some of these issues.

1. Should preparation be "training" or "education"? The position of the Establishment has been that counselors must be "educated," not "trained." Counselor preparation has been lodged in graduate schools requiring all the formal hurdles leading to graduate degrees to be cleared. If in psychology departments, the stress has been on the foundation disciplines. If in schools of education, the content has often been the mastery of "techniques of guidance." On the other hand, beginning with Rogers' assertion that counselors could be *trained* in a few weeks, there has been continual interest in nonacademic *training*. Several reports of successful training of lay therapists in a very brief time are available (Truax and Carkhuff, 1967). The claims for

graduate education have been based on the assumed need for basic knowledge that would give a counselor breadth, flexibility, and the capacity for continued learning and self-development. Rogers (1963) has countered with the position that the very rigidity of graduate education runs counter to the known facts about how people learn, many of which have been gained in the consulting room. The compartmentalization of knowledge, the nature of instruction, and the reward systems are often detrimental to the assimilation of useful knowledge. The issue is clearly represented in the divergence in preparation of a Paterson Ph.D. and one of Truax's lay counselors.

2. Should the focus be on the "personal development" of the counselor or upon his mastery of a body of knowledge and techniques? Related to this is the question of whether counseling is a professional practice or a "way of life." Does a counselor use his knowledge and skill to provide a professional service or is he one more effective person in our society living out his life-style? This issue is in part a variant of the classic argument between the traditionalists and the functionalists. Does behavior change primarily as a result of "knowing" or as a result of "experiencing"? Perhaps it goes deeper than that. Counseling is an act—an interpersonal behavior. Interpersonal behavior is learned, not in the abstract, but through experience with others. At the same time effective counseling has a content that goes beyond the interaction of counselor and client to include extra-counseling client behaviors such as job performance, child rearing, and mating. Part of a counselor's effectiveness depends upon what he does, part on what he knows; yet some counselor educators have acted as though one or the other were immaterial.

3. If the learning central to the counseling process takes place in an atmosphere of minimum threat, isn't the same thing true of the learning central to becoming a counselor? Those who see the relationship and interpersonal behaviors as the alpha and omega of counseling voice a strong affirmative to this question. On the other hand, those who emphasize the content of counseling recognize that evaluation (synonymous to threat for

many) is essential so that the counselor is not allowed to impart inaccurate information, inappropriately interpret tests, or otherwise ineffectively handle the counseling relationship.

4. Should a prospective counselor be taught one systematic approach or be exposed to many with encouragement to select (or construct) an approach that fits him? Some have argued that one of the effective ingredients in counseling is the counselor's *belief* in his system. Indoctrinating a student in one system heightens his belief and makes his approach more integrated. Wide exposure to several points of view decreases the counselor's belief in and reliance on one system. There is ample evidence that all systems get positive results. Some have argued that if a number of counseling theories were examined, the effective elements common to all could be found. This hope of finding the necessary and sufficient conditions for effective counseling has not been especially productive to date. There is not enough time in a graduate program to provide for systematic exposure to a single theory in depth *and* extensive acquaintance with many theories. Therefore the dilemma remains: a single integrated theory or an adequate knowledge of a variety of theories?

5. Who is the best source of feedback regarding counseling effectiveness, clients or supervisors? Most counselor education programs rely mainly on the judgment of supervisors or peers. What is "effective" is dependent upon the supervisor's model or the existing dogma of what counseling should consist of. This obviously differs radically from supervisor to supervisor, as was dramatically demonstrated by Evraiff (1963). Vance in the present volume reflects this condition as he emphasizes the need for experience in a variety of settings with many different supervisors. Clearly, supervisors do not agree on what effective counseling is. Why not turn to the client as a source of information about the effects of counseling? He ought to be able to tell us what helps and what does not—or at least when he has been helped and when he has not—better than supervisors who cannot agree among themselves on a definition of good counseling. Most counseling is in some way built on the assumption that clients can be trusted. We trust them to "help themselves,"

"tell us what they need," "grow," "do what is best for them at the moment." However, the awareness of the "hello-goodbye" effect has caused such widespread distrust of client feedback that no reliable methods have been developed to utilize this source of information in training programs.

The five issues have a seemingly common polarity. Theorists who emphasize empirical approaches to the accumulation of knowledge and its dissemination tend to see counselor education as rational rather than experiential, as education rather than training, as requiring carefully evaluated controlled growth rather than allowing self-development, as containing a body of knowledge and techniques universally applicable in counseling rather than depending on individual counselor approaches, and as relying on supervisor knowledge rather than client feedback. Theorists at the other pole emphasize the experiential, self-development, and the importance of individualized approaches or theories of counseling.

Research Evidence

Unfortunately, the knowledge to resolve many of these issues is not available. We have not been able to answer the critical questions about counseling effectiveness which must be answered before the related questions about counselor preparation can be attacked. Both are ultimately questions of social learning that have definite time linkages. That is, a *given* educator-student interaction in a *given* situation in the preparation phase results in a set of counselor behaviors with a particular client at a particular time which have certain outcomes. We have not yet very successfully identified the counselor behaviors which are linked to particular counseling outcomes. We have rather tended to rely on certain general attitudes and/or behaviors to produce what are viewed as general outcomes. The inability specifically to link counselor behaviors with specific counseling situations has been both cause and effect in our ambiguous and "soft" thinking about counseling. We have relied upon random effects within an ambiguous relationship for "something good" to happen. Our belief that "something good" does happen has limited our research to looking for global outcomes from unspecified processes. One reason for this uncertain status is the complexity of the interaction; careful research of the process requires that counselor characteristics, client characteristics, and situational variables, all of almost infinite variety, be specified. This is an almost impossible research task. But another reason is lack of rigor in the reporting of research. Serkin (1967), in an attempt to examine outcome research reported in the literature, found that she could not easily identify such things as type of training, length of training, amount of experience, or sex of counselor. She also had difficulty in identifying client characteristics, types of problems, length of treatment, or procedures used. Ignoring such critical variables in research reports would not be tolerated in any other profession. A plausible explanation of the extensive contradictory reports of counseling outcomes may be the inadequacy with which the crucial variables have been described and reported.

Even with the complexity of the interaction and the lack of scientific rigor with which investigations of counseling have generally been conducted or reported, some useful conclusions are emerging. Three recent comprehensive reviews of the research literature have been published (Bergin, 1966; Stieper and Wiener, 1965; Truax and Carkhuff, 1967). Though the data are approached from divergent theoretical positions, some common or similar conclusions were reached in these three reviews.

1. Counseling, on the average, is not more helpful than no counseling. Beginning with Eysenck's extensive review and critique of interview therapy, this conclusion has been examined and re-examined. It now seems that, as stated, the evidence favors Eysenck's position, but for different reasons from those that he formulated. A more careful analysis of the data suggest alternative explanations:

a. Many control subjects seek and receive nonprofessional assistance and make gains equivalent to those made by experimental clients. Their gains not only mask the gains made by the experimentals but seriously challenge the *spontaneous remission* argument. At the same time they raise the basic question of the nature of help provided by nonprofessional persons and result in a conclusion that *the conditions for desirable change exist outside professional counseling.*

b. Though the average gains made by control subjects and experimental subjects are equal, the dispersion of gains is greater for experimental subjects. This strongly suggests that some clients get better from counseling and some clients get worse. Since there are now sufficient studies in which experimental and control subjects were equivalent to begin with, it would appear that the counselor influenced the negative as well as the positive changes.

Inference. The behavior of the counselor *is* crucial to client change. Stieper and Wiener refer to the therapist as one of the "power factors" in counseling. As Wrenn (1951) suggested, some persons have enough know-how without training to be effective and some persons with training are ineffective. Training, then, must consist, in part, of the identification of those effective behaviors the person already has and the development of possible additional competences. Bergin stresses the emotional adjustment of therapists, pointing out that there are no data to support the contention that therapy for counselors can substitute for a basically sound personality. Wrenn (1951) concluded that the personality characteristics necessary for effective counseling exist *prior* to training and must be taken into account in selection. The accumulation of data supports that conclusion. There is also some evidence that experience contributes to effectiveness, though it is not sufficient to counter the basic conclusion that some counselors, with or without formal training, are effective and some are not. Watley's (1966) data, though specific to the predictive function of counselors, clearly support this general inference.

2. There are identifiable and operationally definable counselor attributes which seem to have wide applicability in all counseling situations. Truax and Carkhuff refer to them as the "core condition." A growing body of research indicates that the conditions of (a) accurate empathy, (b) nonpossessive warmth, and (c) counselor congruence facilitate client movement while

the absence of these conditions inhibits such growth. As Blocher mentions in his paper, other labels may be applied to these conditions, and, as Bergin suggests, the data are neither conclusive nor equally applicable to all the constructs; but there is so much evidence from a variety of sources that it cannot be ignored.

Inference. To a certain extent, the issue of a single- versus a multiple-theory approach is helped by the above data. Apparently all counselors must possess the capacity for the development of behaviors which bring about these conditions in the counseling relationship. Training programs must be organized to facilitate and evaluate counselor progress on these dimensions whether the same labels are used or not.

3. Even though these core conditions seem necessary, there is evidence that they are not sufficient. Stieper and Wiener (1965) identify one of the power factors as "concrete goal setting" (pp. 126–127):

> . . . Perhaps another major reason why this potentional power factor has not been more adequately explored is that, for the past half century or so, psychotherapists have emphasized their idiosyncrasies. They have devised a plethora of nebulous and sentimental goals for psychotherapy. . . . The damage this kind of vague goal can do to therapeutic *practice* as distinguished from theorizing only . . . is enormous. This kind of misty target can lead to years of meandering in psychological exploration which never really "arrives" anywhere because it did not have a concrete target in the first place. Even worse, teaching students such amorphous "purposes" gives them words and invented concepts which substitute for the evidence of their own ears and eyes about their daily clinical experiences.

As counseling becomes goal specific, it requires concrete knowledge about how to achieve the goals. Developing a compatible marriage and making a vocational decision require different knowledges and behaviors. Helping a student learn effective study behavior calls for different counselor knowledge and skill from those he needs for the working through of parental hostility toward children. Borreson's data (1965) strongly suggest that because of either counselor competence or preference the "developed" problems in counseling are more a function of the counselor than the client. The counselor apparently sets goals and works toward them whether they are explicitly stated or not.

Inference. A counselor must develop the ability to define clearly a particular client's goals and the necessary competences to work toward them or decline the request for help. It is clear that not all counselors are able to help with all problems. Part of the responsibility of a training program must be to help the counselor identify what he can do effectively, strengthen that, and, within the program limits, broaden the range of effective behaviors.

4. There is clear agreement among all three reviewers that the most fruitful future source of information for counselors is the learning laboratory. This stems from the recent work of social learning theorists and applications of more traditional S-R and operant models. More generally it stems from a recognition that counseling is concerned with changing behavior of various kinds and that the basic process is learning. Partly in order to establish ourselves as a profession, we have separated from teachers and others who have been the primary consumers of applied learning theory. There is now a general turning back to education as a basic model for counseling. Some of the models thus far have precipitated intense heat over some sacred cows of counseling such as human freedom and self-actualization. These are no doubt important but not irresolvable issues. The point is that counseling is learning—people can be helped to learn (can be taught?). The source of more effective counseling is probably going to be adaptation of existing and discoverable principles of learning to individual development.

Inference. The evidence is clear that the relationship variables are facilitators of client growth. However, the introduction of specific content (such as vocational or marital information) is not precluded. Neither is the application of particular learning principles (such as reciprocal inhibition or positive reinforcement) to the counseling relationship in order to achieve specific concrete goals agreed upon by the client and the counselor.

It is entirely possible that attempts to understand the relationship should be seen as a learning paradigm (Is nonpossessive warmth a positive reinforcer?). More than ever before it seems that a solid foundation in the psychology of learning may hold the key to effective counselor behavior. Krumboltz (1966) has referred to this major change in theoretical thinking as the *Revolution in Counseling*.

5. Because of the extensive research on expectancy states and client susceptibility to persuasion (see Frank, 1961), there is reason to believe that the change we have attributed to the counseling process and to counselor effectiveness might be better explained by other constructs. One of the hard facts with which counselors must deal is the frequent occurrence of "faith healing" in a variety of forms. At best counseling may be a giant placebo which relies mainly on the client's expectancy of being helped, his susceptibility to persuasion, and the counselor's own belief in his ability to help. At worst counselors may be merely purveyors of their own brand of religion, which has no relevant substance beyond the ability to evoke the faith of the patient in the counselor's ability to help him. It is possible that the three conditions referred to above are primarily means of increasing the counselor's capacity for influence over the client. Stieper and Wiener refer to the therapist as a "Prime Mover" and the most important power factor in therapy.

There is a difference between the effectiveness and the rationale for effectiveness. As professional counselors, we have a social obligation not only to be effective counselors but also to make clear to ourselves and to our public the *basis* of our effectiveness. If counseling is effective persuasion with an irrelevant construct system, then the focus of our efforts should be on identifying the relevant constructs. If, on the other hand, our concepts about individual development are sound, we need to focus on the means of increasing our power to use them to promote the individual's growth.

Inference. The major argument for firmly tying counselor education to graduate education is the need for careful scrutiny of the constructs and methodology of counseling and *not* the

need to teach a fixed system of counseling. It is incumbent upon
a counselor, or at least a reasonable percentage of the profession,
continually to assess the impact of his behavior and to formu-
late adequate explanations of the observed phenomena. Graduate education has as a primary goal the development of the
knowledge and skill to carry out the investigation.

With such general convictions the counselor education faculty
at Minnesota has been attempting to develop a "theory" which
can furnish a guide both to research in counselor education and
to the program of experiences needed to produce effective counselors. Blocher was largely responsible for the current formulation of the construct of multiple response modes which structured the seminar and which he has developed in his paper.
The beginnings are found in his book (Blocher, 1966). The
present formulation was an outgrowth of an advanced seminar
taught jointly with the present author. Recognizing that effective
counseling is (a) a highly personal utilization of oneself, (b) the
wise application of constructs about human development and
behavior from a variety of theories, and (c) the ability to build
continuously upon past experience, he reasoned that a preparation program must contain experiences that will demand the
development of all three capacities in an effective counselor.
To say more than this would be to steal the thunder from his
paper!

The Beginning

Thus the format of the seminar was clear. The three dimensions suggested are associated with prominent "schools" of
thought in counseling, although the wording that has been used
in presenting them may not be the same.

The *existentialists* have stressed the importance of "personal"
involvement, confrontation, and encounter. Rogers' (1961)
On Becoming a Person is a prototype of this position. The assumption seems to be that positive growth is the automatic result of spontaneous, noncognitive, interpersonal experience. Associated with the position is the related T-group training, which
has grown very rapidly in recent years under the sponsorship
and direction of both the Western Behavioral Sciences Institute

and the National Training Laboratories. We have assumed that an exponent of this view would want the counselor education program to place a heavy reliance on the experiential as opposed to the academic and that he could present the thesis that this is *the* approach to counseling and *the* preparation for it. *Jack Gibb,* an early leader in research on small groups, one of the founders of NTL, and more recently associated with the Western Behavioral Sciences Institute, prepared the paper "The Counselor as a Role-Free Person" for this position.

Though there have been counseling theories which have been more rationally oriented than affectively oriented, *cognitive theorists,* as such, are less plentiful. A variety of personality theories, learning theories, and measurement concepts furnish the content of counselor education programs, but theories focusing on the cognition of the counselor per se have received so little attention that Patterson (1966) did not consider them important enough to include in the summary chapter of his comprehensive text, *Counseling Theories. Leon Levy,* a former student of George Kelly's, has been developing a position with regard to cognition as it affects behavior (1963). He consented to prepare his paper "Fact and Choice in Counseling and Counselor Education: A Cognitive Viewpoint" within a relatively short time.*

The necessity for the counselor to use his own experience as ← a basis for testing his constructs and thus improving his performance is closely allied to the D. G. Paterson tradition of *"dust bowl"* empiricism. *Forrest Vance,* a D. G. Paterson student, familiar with the philosophy of science and a strong advocate of empiricism (see Vance, 1964), asserts in his paper that counseling is really learned in the consulting room by seeing a huge variety of clients under many different conditions and very carefully observing the results. From the beginning, *Donald Blocher* saw the need to integrate these three counselor modes of behavior. His paper is an attempt to show both the need for integration and ways of proceeding to ensure it.

Thus, we have four approaches to counselor education: the spontaneous-intuitive, with its emphasis on direct encounter and

* Dr. George Kelly had consented to prepare a paper for the seminar but his sudden illness and death prevented his completion of the task.

confrontation resulting in personal and group responsibility for what is learned as a counselor candidate; the cognitive-conceptual, with its emphasis on the client's personal construct system to be achieved by courses in philosophy of science and theory construction; the hypothesis testing-pragmatic, with its emphasis on supervised practice and internships to be integrated with a minimum of theory; and a new eclecticism, which demands a careful integration of all three.

The force of the seminar was provided by the structure: each paper was answered by a paper propounding an antithetical approach to counselor education. There were eight papers in all. As Bordin had suspected, the discussants were selected with a view to controversy. Because we wanted as thorough a review as possible of each position, each presenter was asked to name several persons who were familiar with his position but not likely to agree with it. *Harold Pepinsky*, an empiricist and a long-time friend of Jack Gibb, took on the task of identifying the role *prescription* outlined in Gibb's paper; *C. H. Patterson*, clearly identified with client-centered relationship therapy, adequately lessened the *dissonance* created by Levy's strong cognitive orientation; *Edward Bordin*, a psychoanalytically oriented counselor, prepared the reaction to Vance's paper (Bordin became ill at the last moment and was unable to attend the seminar. *Dr. Jerome Bach*, a psychiatrist, substituted for Bordin in the discussion); and *Charles Truax*, another avowed eclectic, responded to Blocher's position.

In order to maximize discussion, all the papers were prepared and published in advance of the seminar. The entire time was devoted to a discussion of the material read in advance. Some sessions were structured, but much of the talk was informal, at the dinner table, over coffee, or in rooms late into the night. The major sessions began with the presenter and discussant in dialogue, including the rest of the participants (about forty-five altogether) as time went on. By the last session all formalities had been dispensed with, and discussion took place in round-table fashion.

The format of this monograph is an attempt to catch that flavor. The papers are presented with a summary of the discussion most relevant to them. Obviously, the intensity and verve of the "encounter and confrontation" are lessened to all except those who were present in the experience. We hope the flavor has been preserved.

It is also hoped that the result provides a beginning direction for counselor education, possibly one which has the makings of a theory. Research on the outcomes of such a program is difficult but, we are convinced, crucial to the next stage of development of professional counseling. A model has been built, and the next job is the painful one of subjecting it to stress and identifying the flaws that appear. Then a *better* model can be built.

References

Bergin, A. E.   Some implications of psychotherapy research for therapeutic practice. *Journal of Abnormal Psychology*, 1966 71, 235–246.

Blocher, D. H.   *Developmental Counseling*. New York: Ronald Press, 1966.

Bordin, E. S.   Curiosity, compassion and doubt: The dilemma of the psychologist. *American Psychologist*, 1966, 21, 116–121.

Borreson, Ann.   Counselor influences on diagnostic classification of client problems. *Journal of Counseling Psychology*, 1965, 12, 252–258.

Brammer, L. N., and Shostrum, E. L.   *Therapeutic Psychology*. Englewood Cliffs, N.J.: Prentice-Hall, 1960.

Evraiff, William.   *Helping Counselors Grow Professionally, A Casebook for School Counselors*. Englewood Cliffs, N.J.: Prentice-Hall, 1963.

Ford, D. H., and Urban, H. B.   *Systems of Psychotherapy*. New York: Wiley, 1963.

Frank, J.   *Persuasion and Healing*. Baltimore: Johns Hopkins Press, 1961.

Glasser, W.   *Reality Therapy*. New York: Harper & Row, 1965.
Hewer, Vivian.   The training of psychologists for young adults. Mimeographed, 1966.

Krumboltz, J. D. *Revolution in Counseling*. Boston: Houghton Mifflin, 1966.

Levy, L. *Psychological Interpretation.* New York: Holt, Rinehart & Winston, 1963.

Patterson, C. H. *Theories of Counseling and Psychotherapy.* New York: Harper & Row, 1966.

Rogers, C. R. The necessary and sufficient conditions for therapeutic personality change. *Journal of Counseling Psychology,* 1957, *21,* 95–103.

Rogers, C. R. *On Becoming a Person.* Boston: Houghton Mifflin, 1961.

Rogers, C. R. Graduate education in psychology: A passionate statement. Mimeographed, circa 1963.

Serkin, Sandra. The effects of experimental methodology in counseling outcome studies. Master's paper, University of Minnesota, 1967.

Stieper, D. R., and Wiener, D. V. *Dimensions of Psychotherapy.* Chicago: Aldine, 1965.

Truax, C. B., and Carkhuff, R. R. *Toward Effective Counseling and Psychotherapy: Training and Practice.* Chicago: Aldine, 1967.

Tyler, Leona. Theoretical principles underlying the counseling process. *Journal of Counseling Psychology,* 1958, *5,* 3–10.

Vance, F. L. Folklore, description and science in student personnel work. Unpublished paper, University of Colorado, Division of Student Affairs, 1964.

Watley, D. J. Counselor variability in making accurate predictions. *Journal of Counseling Psychology,* 1966, *13,* 53–62.

Wrenn, C. G. *Student Personnel Work.* New York: Ronald Press, 1951.

2

The Counselor as a Role-Free Person

JACK R. GIBB
La Jolla, California

I believe that one way for a counselor to contribute to the effectiveness and growth of another person is to build a deeply personal, "role-free" relationship with him. This kind of relationship is in itself therapeutic and growth producing. Its helpfulness is limited only by the current capability of the counselor to achieve the personal relationship in sufficient depth and authentic role freedom.

Not all counselors have the ability to achieve such a relationship with others at first, but each one can learn to do so. The education of a counselor should center around his learning to be intensely personal in life situations, particularly in individual and group counseling settings, with the range of persons who come to him for help.

Counseling as Growth

Counseling is the process of restoration or acceleration of growth. Growth by definition is directional movement. For me, the direction is (1) toward trust and personal relationships and away from fear and impersonal relationships, (2) toward open and away from closed behavior, (3) toward self-realization and away from impositional behavior, and (4) toward interdependence and away from dependence. (See Table 1.) All relationships are potentially growth inducing. To the degree that anyone (parent, friend, counselor, manager) is trusting, open, realizing, and interdependent, he is contributing to his own growth and to the growth of the other person.

As they grow, people are continually confronted with four life issues which parallel the four aspects of growth: How much can I trust myself and the world and how personal can I be? How intimate and open can I be? What do I want out of life that will enrich my becoming? How do I influence my world and become a free being? Life is the process of continual confrontation and resolution of these issues. They are never in any sense finally resolved in the person. The effective counselor can achieve a relationship with another that will facilitate the continuing resolution of these issues *in himself and in the other person.* Only as growth (as defined above) occurs in both the counselor and the other person is the relationship truly effective. The counselor and the other person are partners in seeking, confronting, exploring, resolving, and learning to be role free.

Growth is facilitated by high-trust, nondefensive inner conditions and by high-trust, deeply personal relationships. It occurs inevitably in relationships that are personal-trusting, open and intimate, reciprocally fulfilling, and emergently interdependent. (See Table 2.) It is inevitably inhibited in defensive relationships. Defensive (countergrowth) relationships are initiated and/or sustained to ward off perceived or anticipated threat. They are characterized by high fear, masking, persuasion, and dependence. (See Table 3.)

It follows, then, that counselor education should be a process whereby individuals can learn to be more trusting, personal, role free, and warm and less fearful, defensive, and impersonal; to be more intimate, empathetic, intuitive, aware, and confronting and less cautious, deceptive, game-playing, and circumventive; to be more searching, actualizing, and assertive and less manipulative, persuasive, and impositional; and to be more interactive, participative, and interdependent and less dominative, submissive, and managerial. The counselor learns to trust himself, other persons, and the process of growth. He learns to get quickly in touch with his inner feelings, immediate perceptions, and cognitive insights. He learns to share all these with his co-searcher. This process of sharing is best when it is intuitive, but it can also be a deliberate process somewhat under the control of the persons in the relationship.

The intuitive counselor uses his total self as the counseling medium—including particularly his primitive, naïve feelings, perceptions, and cognitions. He brings himself to the relationship. He is present, available, personal, intimate, interdependent, in process, changing, relatively role free, emotional, impulsive, and deeply *with* the other person. As he achieves the capability of being *available* as a person, he inevitably releases feelings of warmth, caring, freedom, and involvement *in himself* and *in the other person*. The counseling situation, then, becomes increasingly therapeutic for and fosters growth in all those involved in it. The counselor ceases to be effective if he ceases to grow in the relationships.

The counselor grows with the counseling. With each personal encounter he becomes more fully a person and more effective as a counselor.

On Being Personal

My own experiences in the field of counseling have been largely in group therapy, group counseling, sensitivity training, and counselor training. I have had only a limited amount of experience in doing individual counseling and therapy.

Over the years I have used several different theories and several different styles of counseling. One effect of these varied approaches has been an increased insight into my own behavior in the counseling situation. I have placed myself in a number of experimental situations in which data of various kinds have been gathered on my behavior and on the behavior of the others during and following the counseling. Thus I have developed considerable confidence in the theory described in this paper. I see myself as primarily a theorist. During the past two years I came to feel that I was most effective when I was not "in role." That is, when I was deliberately trying to help someone, to be a counselor, to "take a stance," to intervene, or to carry out a theory, I felt I was somehow truncating and thus impairing the very relationship that I was trying to achieve. At the same time, in trying to build a simplified and functional theory of the helping relationship, I discovered that a logical derivation from my theorizing produced a similar conclusion to the one stated above. It is impossible for me to tell whether the experiencing or the theorizing came first, or which one produced the other. Increasingly my experiencing and my theorizing are consonant. I believe I am aware of the dangers in such a process and of the historical safeguards that have been created for validating such theories.

I believe that each counselor must, in a sense, create his own theory. He must behave in a way that "fits" him. At the moment I also believe that this role-freedom theory would fit all counselors who gave it a prolonged and role-free trial. That is, the theory is generalizable to all counselors. My experiences in counselor education—in observing counselors in action in group counseling—indicate clearly that counselors who deeply enter the intensive group (as participant or counselor) tend to move toward greater role freedom and toward greater personalness in relationships, regardless of the theory they espouse on joining the group.

Entering the counseling situation (or any interpersonal relationship) with the intention to be personal and to "hang loose," rather than to be role bound or theory bound, seems to make a great deal of difference in what happens to the relationship. Observers in experimental situations and friends in life situations report that I have changed a great deal during the past two years since internalizing the concept of role freedom. I feel more available than I have ever felt before, happier in a wider range of situations, and more able to be *with* others. Along with these changes has come a greater feeling of being helpful in counseling situations. When I relate to others with the intention of being deeply *with* the other person and with the intention of getting personal enrichment from the relationship, I find that I am being more helpful. In effect, I am a better counselor than when I was trying to be one!

I have had some difficulty in communicating what I mean by being personal and role free. A list of some of the signs I look for in attempting to determine whether a counselor is being personal, as I observe him in a counselor education program, may be helpful to the reader.

1. *Closeness to internal reality.* I am personal when I am able to express to another whatever phenomenal reality is available to me at any given moment. To be impersonal is to move toward peripheral areas of awareness, away from central areas of the person.

2. *Face validity of the message.* I am personal when I am able to show my inner feelings clearly to the other, with minimal contamination of the message by masked or distorted expressive habits. To be impersonal is to camouflage my message by deliberate or unconscious-habitual masking, by humor, formality, complexity, deflection, or other indirections.

3. *Clarity of motivation.* I am personal when I can spontaneously reveal my motivation in the process of giving my message. When my depth motivation is closely related to what it seems to me is my message I am being role free. To be impersonal is to attempt to clean up my motivations in the presentation, or to hide my motivations, or to habitually distort them.

4. *Spontaneity and freedom from planned or habitual strategy.* I am personal when I am impulsive, emergent, and spontaneously open, and when I am seen to be so. Psychological distance is created by planning a strategy of approach, by programming my message output, by anticipating what I will do in the counseling session. Those who are close to their intuitions and their "gut feelings" are relatively free of role prescriptions or programming.

5. *Freedom from role.* I am personal when I am responding more to my personal needs than to role demands, responsibilities, and expectations. Duties, expectations, and external demands lead to impersonal role behavior. I cannot be personal when I am consciously or unconsciously being a father, counselor, teacher, helper, or lover. Awareness of role responsibilities is distancing and reduces intimacy.

6. *Freedom from role perceptions.* I am personal when I am able to see the other person as a person and not "in role." I treat the other as a nonperson to the degree that I categorize, box, or reify. Barriers are built when I see him as sick, as in the category of those who need help or treatment, as a child, as an older person, as a client, or as a lawyer. People and events flow, emerge and have unique quality. It may be necessary in the processes of science or understanding to codify, dichotomize, or

simplify. Counseling is a life process and is diminished if one of the participants becomes an observer.

7. *Immediacy of response to another's need or state.* I am personal when I am able to respond impulsively and with minimal contamination to my perceptions of the other person's inner state, and when I am thus validly seen as in tune with the other individual's person. Intimacy is reduced when I delay my response, program my reactions, barter my affections, or hide my angry reactions.

8. *Availability of humanness.* I can be personal when I show my apparent vulnerabilities, emotions, strengths, preferences, secrets, sins, and the other stuff of my inner being. To be impersonal is to attempt to present my better self, my counselor self, my best foot, or to cover my unattractive parts.

9. *Focus on relationships.* I am personal when I am willing and able to enter into a relationship of intimacy, warmth, and I–Thou-ness; to share my feelings about and perceptions of *the relationship.* In order to be able to enter a healing and fulfilling relationship it is not enough to be a person, one must be able to be personal. Being a person and being personal are very different processes. One can be a person without being personal. At the deepest level one is impersonal when he focuses upon his own person or upon the person of the other. An alternating focus is not the same as *being with.* In my work with counselors I find a number who have never experienced what it is like to *be with* another person. To experience this for the first time in counselor education makes for a revealing and dramatic change in insight.

10. *Being here, now.* I can be personal when I can be deeply immersed in the present moment with another or with others who share the moment with me. To be impersonal is to leave the other person and talk about or live in the past, the future, or another place.

11. *Assuming a "with" relationship.* I am personal when I am able to be emergent and interdependent. To be impersonal is to dominate or to submit.

12. *Enjoyment of physical and psychological closeness.* To be personal is to deeply enjoy sustained periods of intimacy with a wide range of persons. Ambivalence about intimacy leads to movement away from personal relationships. I have recently observed many subtle relationships between comfort with sustained physical intimacy and comfort with being psychologically personal. I am coming to feel that a counselor can get great benefit from nonverbal communication and body movement experiences as these are now being developed in therapy and human-potential training.

13. *Preference for concrete and affective communications.* I can be personal when I am concrete and specific and when I am close to my feelings and emotions. To be impersonal is to move toward abstractions and toward being cognitive. Much intellectualization is avoidance behavior. When a person becomes deeply comfortable with his feelings, he tends to prefer and to move toward the feeling component of a relationship and away from the ideational component. A person is never an abstraction. A role always is an abstraction.

14. *Commitment to the other person.* I can be personal to the extent that I can commit myself to the other person. To be impersonal is to avoid commitment. It is my observation that being personal carries with it a commitment. For me it is impossible to be personal without a resultant concern for the other person, an identification, an empathy, and a commitment to him.

The Growth Processes

In the normal processes of growth persons are confronted with sets of recurring concerns, outlined initially in my definition of growth. Growth consists of increased resolution of these concerns. One set of concerns has to do with *acceptance* and *membership.* (See Table 1.) Persons and groups are concerned with the acceptance of self, the acceptance of others, the development of trust, the reduction of fear, the achievement of satisfying membership in relevant groups. The acceptance concern is antecedent to the following three concerns.

A second set of concerns has to do with *intimacy* and *decision*

Basic Modal Concerns	Derivative Personal and Interpersonal Problems	Directions of Personal Growth	Directions of Dyadic Growth
Climate	*Membership:* (How do I learn to trust myself and others, and gain satisfying membership in significant groups?)	*Trust:* (Toward trust and acceptance of self and others; more trust and less fear of persons and of nature)	*Trust:* (Toward a climate of trust and support, low defense and low fear)
Data flow	*Decision Making:* (How do I reveal me, and how do we process feeling and perception data into valid decisions?)	*Openness:* (Toward greater awareness and reception, more valid output, open spontaneity)	*Openness:* (Toward a more valid feedback system and consensual decision making)
Goal formation	*Productivity:* (How do I find out who I am and what I want, and how do we find out what to seek, produce, and work for?)	*Realization:* (Toward self-fulfillment and actualization; goal integration; self-determination and self-assessment)	*Realization:* (Toward an integration of dyadic goals, dyadic determination, and dyadic assessment of progress)
Control	*Organization:* (How do I find an inner, emergent control and value system, and how do we achieve a functional interdependence?)	*Interdependence:* (Toward an emergent integration of values and ability to take a "with" relation)	*Interdependence:* (Toward an emergent norm and control system, a participative interdependence)

Table 1 *Directions of Growth in the Person and in the Counselor-Person Dyad*

making. These concerns are about communication with self and others, intimacy and psychological distance, role and personness, authenticity, understanding and being understood, and the processing of these data into group decisions. This set is intertwined with the membership concern and can be satisfyingly dealt with only when some genuine processing of the membership concern has occurred.

A third set of concerns has to do with *motivation* and *productivity*. It relates to motivation, purpose, personal identity, self-actualization, group goal setting, and the influencing of the goals of others. This set is best dealt with after some progress has been made on the membership and intimacy concerns.

A fourth set of concerns has to do with *control* and *organization* and relates to authority, freedom, control, interdependence, rebellion, and cooperation. It is clearly contingent upon development among the three other major concerns.

In the model I am presenting the counselor enters the relationship in a very personal way. He comes to see the dyad as a two-person exchange rather than as a role-role relationship. He shares his naïve impressions of the other's concerns about acceptance, intimacy, identity, and potency. As these concerns arise, he shares his current feelings of defense (fears about being unhelpful, irritation at the other's presenting behavior, etc.), feelings about façade and intimacy (distrust of what the other is saying, his own ambivalence about getting more close, his own need for intimacy), feelings about goals and motivations (sense of the other's resistance or apathy, his own feelings of fulfillment or achievement, etc.), and feelings about influence and authority (feelings about being unable to influence the other, his own resistance to attempts by the other to influence him, etc.). I do not mean to suggest that the counselor programs or plans these feelings and expressions. They occur inevitably as he learns to enter a relationship with the intention of being personal.

The more readily the counselor can make available current and valid feelings and perceptions, the more personal and intimate the relationship becomes. The counselor is most helpful when he can shed his role prescriptions, live in the existential present, articulate his immediate and primitive feelings as they occur, enter the other's emotional world, and become truly interdependent.

Trusting the Process—Working in this intuitive-personal mode, at least as I am viewing it from here, requires a high degree of trust on the part of the counselor. It is necessary to *trust the process* and not try to steer it. I am most effective as a counselor when I enter into the relationship to learn, share, grow, experience deeply, feel, act, relate, learn about myself, work together on problems, search, and emerge. I am least effective when I come into the relationship to teach, help, guide, counsel, model, remedy, advise, coach, mold, steer, fix, correct, train, or do therapy. If I *genuinely* and deeply come into the relationship in order to grow and to enrich myself, the other person in the joint venture also grows. Thus I incidentally fulfill my professional role responsibilities, as defined in the conventional sense. That is, the other person does grow, learn, and become more effective.

From experience I *know* that the four concerns will arise, that significant progress and work on the concerns will *inevitably* take place, that deeply personal relationships are therapeutic per se, that growth will result, and that loving and caring will occur between us. That is what I mean by trusting the process. This fact has significance for the training of counselors. It is necessary for the counselor to gain this trust through experience so that he deeply knows he will be effective. He must know that he is unique, that his intuitive responses will have increasing validity, that he will be helpful, and that growth will occur.

My wife Lorraine and I, as co-theorists, have developed a viewpoint that is relevant here. We have postulated two sets of processes which go on in both the person's intrapersonal and his interpersonal environment. Under one set of hypothetical conditions he develops a trusting orientation toward the world, makes trust assumptions about people, and is predisposed to build growth relationships as described in Table 2. Under the other set of internal and external conditions he develops a fear orientation toward the world, makes fear-distrust assumptions about people, is predisposed to defend himself, takes counter-growth attitudes, and builds the defensive relationships described in Table 3.

In our system trust and fear are antonyms representing polar ends of the central life processes. As a person grows, his trusts become more enduring, more reality based, and more inter-

Basic Modal Concerns	Growth Relationships	Typical Behaviors and Attitudes	Typical Feelings
Climate	Trust-Acceptance: (Reciprocal state of deep trust, caring, and affection)	Acceptance: (Confidence, trust, personal and nonrole relationship, nonjudgmental attitude)	Warmth: (Affection, love, esteem, sympathy, caring)
Data flow	Openness-Intimacy: (Two-way communication in depth; reciprocal empathy and receptivity)	Empathy-Listening: (Rapport, communion; impulse, spontaneity, intimacy)	Intimacy: (Serenity, warmth, freedom, comfort, safety, coziness)
Goal formation	Realization-Search: (Reciprocally fulfilling and shared problem solving and search)	Quest: (Searching, actualizing, fulfillment, achievement, exploring)	Zest: (Eagerness, exhilaration, fervency, satisfaction, well-being)
Control	Interdependence-Emergence: (Participative, emergent and role-free state of interdependent cooperation)	Integration: (Participation, interaction, freedom, spontaneity, cooperation, working with)	Freedom: (Power, importance, worth, adequacy, potency, sense of being needed)

Table 2 *The Growth (Therapeutic) Relationships*

Basic Modal Concerns	Defensive Relationships	Typical Behaviors and Attitudes	Typical Feelings
Climate	*Fear-Distrust:* (Reciprocal state of fear, distrust, high defense)	*Punishment:* (Evaluation, judgment, moralizing, coldness, fear, distrust)	*Alienation:* (Hostility, envy, suspicion, fear, cynicism)
Data flow	*Distance-Façade:* (Reciprocal masking, strategic distancing, superficial communication)	*Strategy:* (Circumvention, masking, distortion, deception, politeness, ambiguity, formality)	*Loneliness:* (Estrangement, withdrawal, depression, sadness)
Goal formation	*Persuasion-Competition:* (Reciprocal imposition, polemic, counterforce, and dissonant locomotion)	*Persuasion:* (Coercion, guidance, manipulation, passivity, resistance)	*Indifference:* (Apathy, disinterest, resentment, latent hostility)
Control	*Dependence-Dominance:* (Differential status and power; dominance countered by submission or rebellion)	*Control:* (Management, dependency, counterdependency, rebellion, submission)	*Impotence:* (Inadequacy, tension, latent or manifest hostility)

Table 3 *The Defensive (Countergrowth) Relationships*

twined with his life theme and life theory. He learns to trust more and fear less. With increasing trust he learns to be more caring, more intimate, more search oriented, and more interdepending. The intuitive-internal mode or stance assumed by the counselor is most congruent with a growth relationship as herein described. In this mode both the counselor and the other person grow. The counselor becomes more personal-trusting, more open-intimate, more reciprocally fulfilling, and more interdependent.

Fear—Table 3 summarizes the countergrowth processes, behaviors, and feelings that arise when fear is the prepotent factor in the momentary or enduring relationship. Fear predisposes one to defend his behavior, attitudes, life theory, and perception of the world. Both participants in the counseling relationship become defensive as they feel themselves threatened by anticipated, imagined, and reinstated fears. The early climate in the counseling dyad is, of course, clearly defensive. It is important to the growth of both the counselor and the other person that each bring out his fears, see how they become transfigured in his life style and his life theory. Because fear reduction is the central dynamic of growth, it is critical in the counseling process to focus upon these fears and their effects. It is my experience that the critical and blocking fears relate to the interpersonal situations, are self-fulfilling, are not based upon social reality, and are augmented by impersonal counseling. Fears are reduced by sustained experience that invalidates them. The most adequate way to reduce these "social" fears is through personal, intimate and intuitive counseling. The counselor must show his own fear and *live with* the client in a two-person or multi-person world, sharing existential crises in their fullness.

Fear predisposes a person to build fear-distrust relationships which inhibit growth. The projections of the fearful counselor contain the punishing, distancing, coercive, and controlling elements in himself. He therefore sees the other person as full of elements that corroborate his fears. Particularly if he has been trained to see disease entities and neurotic symptoms, his anxieties about adequacy and effectiveness will be self-fulfilling. He will see the things he has been trained to see. The counselor who is objective, rational, impersonal, analytical, aloof, and role taking tends to corroborate the fears of the other person and contributes to some degree to the feelings of alienation, loneliness, disinterest, latent hostility, and cynicism that characterize the phenomenological worlds of many who come to him for help.

The fearful person manages, filters, and distorts his communications with himself and with others. He often finds it difficult to recognize his own fears. Fears are fearful. The person who comes to the counselor for help is usually defensive, role ridden, and tends to play the games of defensive strategy. The conventional counselor often inadvertently plays the game of the role-ridden client. The emergent or intuitive counselor refrains from playing the counselor or therapist game and comes as a person to another person. The role is a barrier, a wall, a block to communication, an encapsulation, a formalization that prevents communication and relationships in depth. The person who is in role tends to respond in role and to be responded to in terms of the role expectation by the other. The "counselor" puts on his counselor "hat," chooses a strategy for "intervention," decides on an appropriate temporal sequence for the interview, and together with the "client" develops a strategy for his behavior change. The attitudes which are consonant with this language tend to depersonalize, objectify, and rob the relationship of its potential for enduring growth.

Role behavior is distancing. It is impossible for a "counselor" to communicate in depth with a "client." What I am, deeply and spontaneously, may be communicated in depth to another person if each is relatively free of role, of methods and techniques, of constraining expectations, of titles and categories, of role demands and obligations, of rules and games, of the formal structure that permits roles to relate but prevents persons from relating. It is, of course, not possible for individuals to free themselves completely from role prescriptions and methods. Role prescriptions and methods are artificial abstractions useful for observers in facilitating descriptions of events. However, when participants in the process begin to use the language of role, phrase their alternatives in role language, and communicate to each other in role, they tend to reduce the emergent spontaneity that creates personal relationships.

Fear makes a person susceptible to impositional and persuasive motivation. The person who comes to the counselor for help is often one who, in fear, comes to look outside himself for legitimation of his behavior, sanction for his goals, and validation of his life. He is not comfortable with his inner motives or trusting of his impulses and spontaneous desires. He is predisposed to look for what he ought to do. His reactions to the controls of others range from frenetic compliance to resentful passivity. The conventional or "teaching" counselor to some extent plays the game of the defensive client. Guidance is so embedded in our culture, in our language and practice of counseling, and in the educational settings in which much counseling occurs that it is very difficult to avoid playing the forensic game with the client. Consciously or unconsciously we attempt to teach him our values, our adaptive mechanisms, and our theories. The intuitive counselor, when most effective, avoids much of this persuasion, or at least brings into focus and open awareness his needs to change the client and to manage the client's motivations.

Fear predisposes a person to overperceive and overreact to the significance of authority figures and the importance of management and control. The intuitive counselor deals directly with the authority problem by focusing upon the "here and now" dynamics of the relationship between himself and the other person: reciprocal attempts to deal with influence, control, status, and authority. The intuitive counselor bypasses the historical etiology of the dependency problems and deals directly with present relationships. It may be that at this point the intuitive models are most vulnerable. The analytic theories, presumably best able to analyze dependency, deal most directly with authority problems. Again, it is the current manifestations of reciprocal influence that concern the client. The intuitive counselor works directly with the current and available ways in which the client manifests his needs to exert influence.

Life Styles and Life Theories

The counselor presents himself to a person who has developed a more or less stabilized and enduring life style. This life style comes from a blending of growth experiences and defensive experiences predisposing the person to some mixture of fear and trust. The person's life style, management style, implicit life theory, management theory, defense level, and perceptual system tend to stabilize, accommodate, and develop into a constellation that becomes predictable to himself and to others.

Many phenomena serve to perpetuate and confirm this stable system. The trusting person acts in a trusting way and breeds trust. The fearful person communicates fear and breeds fear and distrust. Behavior thus tends to have a self-fulfilling quality. In a sense, a person produces his own experience.

These phenomena tend to generate in the person a set of rationalizations and implicit assumptions that fit his trust or fear world and become a relatively stable life theory which is highly consonant with his prepotent need system and his stabilized life style. The theory is supported by his need system at many levels. It is difficult for new or disconfirming data to intrude into this stabilized system.

The relevant and central aspects of one's life theory and life style are revealed directly in the counseling interview. The person manages his world, his family, and his life situations in the same manner that he manages his relationships with the counselor. The intuitive counselor who enters the counseling situation as a person comes to deal directly with emerging patterns of being personal, open, realizing, and interdepending. It is our experience (which is largely in personal and group counseling in organizational settings) that these four aspects of the behavior of the person in counseling are very similar to his behavior in the organizational setting, and that with counseling his behavior tends to change in all four aspects. The maintenance of the change is another matter. Behavior change on the job and in the organization is hard to maintain because this person is subjected once again to life styles based on the fear assumptions. Only when the new life style can be sufficiently satisfied in counseling or when the old environment is changed significantly can the new behaviors be maintained.

It is, indeed, this difficulty of making permanent changes in life behavior that leads me to a strong preference for intuitive counseling. If my analysis of life theory is correct, the behavior that is required to adjust to the personal, role-free, and emergent counseling situation is the behavior that is most effective in the job and school setting.

Love—Everyone needs to love and to be loved. In order to sustain growth, man must learn to love himself and he must be loved by others. In the normal interactions in daily life a great many people neither learn to love themselves nor learn to behave in ways that draw love from others.

Role therapy and role relations in our culture are partially effective in supporting or re-establishing growth—partly because even partial or pseudo love is to some extent fulfilling to the love-starved individual. Love given for pay, from pity, from duty, as fulfilling a role expectation, as reassurance to a person perceived as needing it, as a form of guilt reduction, as punishment, as ritual, or in the other multitudinous forms of pseudo love is probably therapeutic and meets the need to some degree. Under these conditions it is always truncated, muted, and robbed of its full effect.

What all deeply need is more genuine, spontaneous, emergent, or personal love. It is more difficult to come by. This kind of love is more rare but more therapeutic and conducive to growth.

A role cannot love a role. One of my deepest convictions and a postulate in our systematic theory is that whenever a *person* relates to another *person* in a personal way love inevitably grows in the relationship. A counselor cannot love a client—but a counselor can learn to be personal and in so doing can learn to love any particular person, can increase his propensity for loving a wide range of persons, and can increase the availability of his loving responses.

The most fundamental reason for the effectiveness of intuitive and personal counseling is that the person needing help can achieve genuine love. Open, direct and honest communication with another necessarily produces a lowering of defense and an emerging love. Punishing, controlling, impersonal, and strategic behaviors are incommensurate with loving behaviors, are defensive in character, and are reduced with deeply personal relationships—in or out of counseling.

In counseling both participants can learn to be more responsive to proffered love. Each can learn to demonstrate love when
he feels it. Each can discover how quickly genuine love can
emerge in a fear-free and defense-free situation. Each can realize
that genuine love need not be frightening. Each can experience
for himself at the deepest level of which he is capable his
"basic" nature. He becomes aware that at his core he is indeed
loving and lovable. All this is not easily achieved because even
the best counselor is not entirely free from fearful, nontrusting
behavior.

Need Systems—The wide prevalence of ambivalent feelings
and the apparent paradoxes in loving-hating behavior have led
us to assume that a person is under the influence of two contrapuntal need systems. (See Table 4.) In interpersonal interaction

Table 4   *Contrapuntal Need Systems in the Person*

Basic Modal Concerns	Growth Needs (ascendant during high-trust, low-fear states)	Defense Needs (ascendant during low-trust, high-fear states)
Climate	*Love:* (To give and receive love and trust)	*Punishment:* (To give and receive punishment, to manage warmth)
Data flow	*Intimacy:* (To give and receive communication in depth, to be intimate)	*Distance:* (To give and receive social distance, to withdraw, to manage intimacy)
Goal formation	*Realization:* (To give and receive personal fulfillment)	*Persuasion:* (To give and receive persuasion-imposition, to manage goals)
Control	*Freedom:* (To give and receive freedom)	*Control:* (To give and receive controls, to be dominant or dependent)

there is always some withdrawal in approach, some hostility in affection, some manipulation in sharing, and some deception in openness. Fear predisposes us to react to the fear component and trust predisposes us to react to the trust component. Growth is a constant polyphonic process of counterbalancing within the organism the needs to love and punish, to be intimate and to withdraw, to fulfill others and to manipulate them, to interdepend and to control.

Under high trust man acts as if he has four dominant needs: to give and receive love, to give and receive intimacy, to give and receive fulfillment, and to give and receive freedom (Table 4). Under high fear-defense he acts as if he has four prepotent needs: to give and receive punishment, to give and receive distance, to give and receive persuasion, and to give and receive control.

There is a large degree of interrelationship in the cluster of high-trust motivations and behaviors and also within the cluster of high-fear motivations and behaviors. An angry, hostile person is likely to attempt to control and to manipulate. Punishment and control are especially related, both in motivation and in expression. The defense system is triggered as a constellation. Manifest and phenotypical behaviors are diverse and complex, depending upon the life style. We are assuming that the need system is mobilized in a genotypically unitary way. Phenotypical diversity masks the underlying unity of the two need systems.

The fear-defense need system mobilizes needs and manifest behaviors that are harmful to the long-range growth needs of the person. Punishment, withdrawal, control, and manipulation are manifest behaviors that meet temporary system requirements. These behaviors are dysfunctional, neurotic, and self-defeating in the sense that they do not meet the long-range needs of the human system. Behavior that is loving, intimate, realizing, and freedom giving is activated by the trust system and is more fundamental and intrinsic to the enduring nature of the organism.

Counselor Education

I am inclined to encourage a great deal of diversity, decentralization, and experimentation in counselor education. Am-

biguity, multiplicity of theory, and great difference in practice
are to be encouraged and are quite suitable to the present state
of the art. There is appropriate risk in encouraging creative ex-
perimentalism. Confrontation and explication of difference,
such as are taking place in this seminar, are helpful and developmental. I should like to see a number of widely diverse programs
of counselor education in operation.

It seems important to me that prospective counselors have
great freedom of choice in developing counseling modes, choosing theoretical frameworks, and experiencing a variety of styles,
theories, and settings. Students should be encouraged to experiment within a wide spectrum at least comparable to the diversity that currently exists among established professionals. We
should promote invention, creativity, and the risk of failure and
professional disapproval.

Each student should be optimally free to develop a theory and
a mode which feels good to him. Counselors are best when they
are doing what they deeply feel is most effective. Personal commitment is a significant variable in counselor success.

Certainly we should foster more hardheaded research on the
problems discussed in this paper. Practice is always far ahead
of research, however, and I would not suggest that creative
theorists or practitioners wait for research. Conceptualization,
empirical research, and "engineering" practice should be inter-
laced and related. At this point in time, with regard to counselor education, particularly in exploring the implications of the
intuitive mode, I believe that what is needed is creative invention, imagination, diversity, speculation, and all sorts of demonstration projects. For me, at least, the issues need refining.

The implications for counselor education of this emergent
model of counseling are fairly clear and direct. The counselor can
learn to be personal and role free in the counseling situation and
in other life situations. He must learn to be personal, open,
present, available, spontaneous, courageous, articulate, confronting, transparent, and relatively free of his role structure.

Achieving Person-ness—More specifically, person-ness is
achieved through experiences which produce greater trust, openness, self-determination, and interdependence. It is probably
not possible, and perhaps not theoretically sound, to program in

advance what kinds of experiences can be expected to produce a
true "person" or bring forth the capability of relating in a "personal" way. I will suggest what seem to me to be some hoped-for
outcomes of the experiences:

1. *Greater trust and less fear.* With depth experience, the
person comes to have greater trust in himself, in others, in the
natural processes of life, in his impulses and own internal life,
and in his capabilities.

2. *Greater capacity to love and to be loved.* The person comes
to care for himself and for others with whom he has contact in
depth. Counselors can and do learn to be more expressive of
their inner feelings. The expression changes the relationship,
which in turn leads to greater expression.

3. *A more effective input system.* The person comes to have
greater empathy, and takes in, with minimal distortion, the feeling and cognition data from the world around him.

4. *A more effective output system.* The person learns to verbalize his feelings and cognitions and to communicate them to
others with minimal distortion. His verbal and nonverbal communications are consonant with his inner states. His messages
are clear.

5. *Intrapersonal communication.* The person comes to know
who he is and what he is becoming. He is aware of his feelings,
he knows what he thinks, he has come close to his inner core, he
finds where he "is at." If the counselor is to use his intuitive being as a medium for counseling, this is a particularly significant
aspect of training. "The medium is the message" is the emergent
theory. That is, the growing relationship is the therapeutic message—not the verbal content of the communications during the
counseling interview.

6. *Interdependence.* The person is able to be intensely with
another person. He finds satisfactions in interdependence. He
feels both free and powerful in relating to others. He can relate

bodily, cognitively, affectively, and in a task situation. Being personal *is a relationship* between persons. Interdependence is the essential nature of the effective counseling relationship and is thus of central importance in the training of the counselor.

7. *Self-determination and self-assessment.* The person comes to some kind of integration of his inner goals. He is moving toward self-actualization and knows that he is and how to assess his progress.

The following is a list of some of the experiences that seem to be helpful in attaining the capability of taking a personal relationship.

1. *Exposure of self.* It is helpful for the person to have a wide variety of experiences in which he opens himself up to the interpersonal world. He must be involved in situations in which he comes operantly to expose his deepest fears, vulnerabilities, loves, and trusts. He must have these exposed to himself and to others.

2. *Experiences of being personal with many kinds of people.* The potential counselor is helped by experiences in depth with a variety of presenting selves, coping mechanisms, cultural differences, psychopathologies, emotions, and media of self-expression.

3. *Confrontation and feedback.* It is helpful for the person to have experience with direct verbal and emotional feedback so that he sees the direct and indirect effects of his behavior upon others. He is helped by being confronted with anger, conflict, love, pain, and other diverse effects of his behavior.

4. *Experience with many counselor styles and modes.* Observation helps. The one-way screen is useful. Films are useful. Direct participation with other counselors as co-therapists is even more helpful. Direct experimentation with many styles (with observation, feedback, and clinical experience with each style) is perhaps still more valuable. The counselor should come to *know*, at a gut level, how it feels to develop a variety of styles.

5. *Experience with a diversity of inner states.* The potential counselor is helped by having direct experience with his own euphoria, grief, loneliness, anger, pain, anguish, hate, love, rejection, and other tough and tender inner states.

6. *The intensive group experience.* It is helpful to be a member, observer, therapist, or co-therapist in a marathon, T-group, analytic therapy session, sensory awareness group, nonverbal group, and other available group experiences that are emerging. I would say that an intensive marathon group, integrated with body movement experiences, is an essential part of the training of a competent counselor. I know of no more effective way of getting the first three experiences mentioned above than an intensive role-free marathon. Counselors who have participated with me in such a training session have reported, without exception, a tremendous change in their counselor behavior and effectiveness.

7. *Theory seminars.* It is probably helpful to have a direct cognitive interchange with knowledgeable people who have well-formulated life theories, management theories, or counseling theories. It is valuable to verbalize, defend, live, and attack the theory. Role playing, clinics, and seminars are sometimes helpful, depending upon the openness of the counselor to such experiences.

8. *Directed "growth" experiences.* It is helpful to have lived a variety of the currently emerging "personal growth potential" experiences: induced meditation, hinge experiences, guided daydreams, peak experiences, psychedelic experiences, physical movement, extended perception, Synanon games, sensory awareness, touching and other nonverbal experiences. I am particularly impressed with touching, nonverbal communication, and sensory awareness as media for removing the barriers to more personal relationships. I believe that all humans have the capacity for being creative and being personal. The functional use of this capacity is a matter of barrier removal and not of training, per se. People do not need to be trained to be personal. When fears are removed, they naturally become personal.

9. *Experience as a counselor.* With or without the help of an experienced co-learner, supervisor, and teacher, there is no substitute for direct individual and group counseling.

10. *Life experiences.* Presumably the person is enriched, deepened, and broadened by life experiences: marriage, parenthood, divorce, teaching, death of a loved one, travel, war, commitment in a mental hospital, living in another home, taking drugs, becoming a homosexual or an alcoholic, preparing for another profession, working in a cannery, joining a monastery, becoming a pacifist, going to Selma, murdering someone, or committing suicide. Lacking some of the above, one can have surrogate experiences: reading novels, watching television, taking field trips, or visiting institutions.

A Model for Counselor Education—As a sample demonstration model for counselor education I would suggest the following program.

A group of sixteen or thirty-two applicants would be selected for the program. The basis for selection would be some assessment of primary commitment to a counseling career. If money were available for assessment, I would have all applicants placed in a six-day marathon T-group and then have an assessment group judge movies of two sample hours of interaction. Judges would select applicants on the basis of estimate of growth potential: capability of being trusting, open, self-determining, and interdependent. From my experience I would assume that there would be high observer agreement.

Either one or two living and learning communities would be formed. These groups of sixteen people, preferably each having eight men and eight women, would form as continuing T-groups for the four years of the professional training program. In addition to having both sexes, it would be helpful to select persons from sharply different socioeconomic, cultural, and family backgrounds.

The group of sixteen persons would be completely free to determine its own goals and activities. It would be advantageous, but not necessary, to have good physical facilities, an excellent library, living quarters nearby for families, an available professional resource staff and money to obtain professional help on request, and perhaps a good convener-secretary-administrator who would be capable and thoroughly committed to the norms, aims, and freedom-trust in the program. It would also be useful to allow the group to solve its own administrative problems without an administrative resource person. This would be a good experience in integrating management theory with life style.

My prediction from considerable experience with T-groups which have endured for several months and several hundred hours is that the T-groups would spend considerable time at first on personal-growth aims. For the first three to six months they would undergo primarily a personal-growth group experience. The group would grow on each of the four dimensions listed in Table 1. It would develop a high degree of membership, trust, affection, and person-ness. It would develop a great deal of openness and increasingly be able to make consensual decisions on all critical action issues. It would create emergent action goals on which there would be consensus. That is, the group would plan activities, bring in resource people, make experiential training designs, building a learning and action community, and do some creative and unpredictable things that would be highly related to the development of professional and personal skills. It would build an interdependent team that would come to have emergent leadership, minimum formal control, and a strong sense of freedom and power. Members would be able to do what they wished as individuals but also would have the strength and skill to undertake interdependent activities that they would not be able to engage in alone. The program would turn out to be far more creative than anything at present available and would lead to significant changes in existing programs.

Table 5 presents what Lorraine Gibb and I have found to be the inevitable experiences that occur in such groups when they stay together over long periods of time. We have called these experiences "TORI experiences" (for trust, openness, realization, and interdependence). They parallel the four modal concerns in our theoretical system and represent enrichments of personal and group living. They always take place in what we have called TORI groups (long-range T-groups that are initially

Table 5 *The TORI Depth Experiences*

Basic Modal Concerns	The TORI Personal-Enrichment Experience	The TORI Group-Enrichment Experiences
Climate	*Trust-Love:* (I feel loved and trusted now and am a lovable person, fully deserving of love and trust)	*Caring:* (All group members have a deep, sustained feeling of trust and love for all members of the group)
Data flow	*Intimacy:* (I feel at this moment completely understood at all levels and feel that I can be again; am relating as a role-free person)	*Consensus:* (Complete group understanding and agreement on a course of action after full exploration of all relevant alternatives in personal, role-free interaction)
Goal formation	*Zest:* (I have found a goal that is deeply mine and gives full meaning and becoming to my life at this moment)	*Commitment:* (Sustained and genuinely zestful search by all members for an enduring, consensual goal)
Control	*Freedom-Power:* (I feel exhilaratingly free and powerful and am not anxious about anyone abridging either my freedom or my power)	*Emergence:* (The emergence of a true constraint-free group interdependence with no rules or status-role hierarchy)

leaderless and that start with initial commitment). It is my prediction that these experiences would occur early in the first year of the counselor education groups and would provide a therapeutic and unprecedentedly rich, growth-promoting experience for each member of the group.

I am also assuming that the group would develop many or all of the hoped-for outcomes listed earlier. A number of studies have shown significant gains on most of these variables from even short-term T-groups of the conventional variety. Other, less predictable and more exciting gains would come from the program too, most of them in the direction of developing greater capability to perform the professional counseling tasks.

Moreover, the work groups would create and select a variety of the experiences listed above in addition to a number of other unpredictable and creative ones. Several models come to mind that contain elements of the above program. I am particularly impressed with Summerhill, with the Esalen Institute intern program at Big Sur, California, and with the experiment in living at KAIROS in Rancho Santa Fe, California. I am increasingly amazed, as I consult with various educational, industrial, religious, hospital, governmental, and volunteer organizations, at the great amount of personal and professional growth that comes from self-motivated people working on self-selected tasks in work or organizational climates that have even a modicum of freedom and trust. A number of pilot and demonstration programs in organizations are under way which already indicate the potential in greater freedom-trust management climates. The management of counselor training has in the past been far too restrictive, conventional, directive, cognitive, and confined to too limited a range of educational activities. I see encouraging signs of freedom, trust, experimentation, and creativity.

I have complete confidence that the potential counselors working in such a program would become more deeply personal and role free in a sense not easily imaginable by those of us who are currently in the field. I find myself becoming more personal and emergent in my own life and in my professional counseling. It seems to me that I have come a long way in my own trust and openness, in the past few years particularly, and I am even more aware of my own potential and how much farther I can go as I move toward more trust, less fear, and more openness. Recent experiences have made me more conscious of the previously unguessed potential in increasing freedom from role and in greater person-ness.

From WHIG to TORI (*sic*)?

HAROLD B. PEPINSKY
The Ohio State University

What Jack Gibb has to say about the counselor as a "role-free" person deserves to be taken seriously. Before it can, however, one must allow himself to become Jack Gibb's student, following him through an elaborate description of a way toward "growth." There are many signposts to watch for here—*vegmerkene* such as Hammarskjold might have sought for to soothe his inner torment had he been less oriented toward Stockholm and more toward the Big Sur. Jack Gibb not only tells his reader from whence he has come but where to go and how to get there. And the proffered reward of personal growth through enabling others to grow is seen to be large indeed. One comes to receive much through his spontaneous acts of giving. By implication, here is the road toward the good life in the good society, of which many of us in America must have dreamed.

Throughout his essay Jack Gibb tells us his own story, ending with a testimonial about how far he has traveled:

> I find myself becoming more personal and emergent in my own life and in my professional counseling. It seems to me that I have come a long way in my own trust and openness, in the past few years particularly, and I am even more aware of my own potential and how much farther I can go as I move toward more trust, less fear, and more openness.

Two essential signs of growth, which Jack Gibb has sought for himself and for others, are specified here: trust and openness. The other two are realization and interdependence. These four components and their attainment comprise what Jack and Lorraine Gibb have articulated as TORI experiences, "inevitable" for groups of persons "when they stay together over long periods of time" in a proper kind of training group environment. Such experiences are shown to "represent enrichments of personal and group living."

Jack Gibb's careful exposition of his idealized actor-and-society, together with how this is to be brought about, evokes compassion and respect. As he describes it, his own struggle toward TORI-hood has been a long and poignant one. And the surcease from pain and bewilderment, the sense of personal enlightenment and dignity even, which his work seems to have afforded himself and others, is all the more remarkable because self-fulfillment is attached to other-fulfillment. With no intended disparagement I wish to point out the similarity between Jack Gibb's message and the messages of great religious movements, such as early Christianity and Buddhism, in the history of mankind. In the case of TORI, as it is expounded in Gibb's paper, a master artisan has made an explicit statement of his creed.

There is also a manifest similarity between Gibb's message and those of Carl Rogers and Abraham Maslow. I am given to understand, however, that Gibb has evolved his own content and style out of his extensive work with groups over the past twenty years. Perhaps it is not surprising that in our time in our country this phenomenon should have occurred. And it is perhaps not surprising that California has provided a locus of activity for all three of these people. In recent years a number of popular magazines have devoted whole issues to that great state and its affairs. The late Frank Lloyd Wright is supposed to have said that once upon a time there occurred in this nation a great western tilt, as the result of which everything that was loose rolled into southern California. Certainly it appears to have become a Mecca for activists, and for restless and troubled spirits of all kinds. Jack Gibb's paper reveals a literally touching concern for establishing instant intimacy with individual members of a horde of mobile strangers.

The gifted young writer Page Stegner has just written a novel that has made clearer for me the world of tormented souls, for whom TORI experiences may well be indicated. His novel *The Edge* (Stegner, 1967) is worth reading in this connection. As the dust jacket states, with rare lack of exaggeration,

> *The Edge* is set in present-day California—Santa Barbara, Big Sur, San Francisco. It is a novel about the edge of our continent and the people who are drawn there in search of some

> kind of salvation . . . about the edge of the mind and its ten-
> dency to crumble . . . about a young man . . . doomed to walk
> the edge of sanity, moral responsibility, and commitment.

I strongly recommend *The Edge* as an accompaniment to Jack
Gibb's chapter in this book. There are persons, miserably lonely
and closed in upon themselves, who may well require for their
salvation what TORI promises. Whether TORI offers its can-
didates more than "reality therapy," "positive fighting," "game"
or "interaction analysis," or a hundred other kinds of therapy
that Californians offer to Californians, is a question that I cannot begin to answer here. Each of these named therapies has
its vigorous and eloquent proponents. So do "behavior therapies" and "chemotherapies," and prescriptions for "community
health."

If I have not chosen to place much credence in Jack Gibb's
"theory" or in his "research findings," it is because the latter
are not given to me in his paper and the former is never stated
in terms that permit of refutation. But he has a perfect right
to call himself a "theorist," his claims do not suffer too much,
by comparison with what others have to offer, for the lack of
"hard data" to support them. Refutable statements about "therapy" have not yet been made; they presuppose a theoretical and
methodological sophistication still to be attained.

The Problem of "Role Freedom"

I am perplexed by many of the terms Jack Gibb uses in his
paper. For example, what does he mean by "role free"? In one
place he tells us that this means "greater role freedom and . . .
greater personalness in relationships." In the next paragraph he
says, "When I relate to others with the intention of being
deeply *with* the other person and with the intention of getting
personal enrichment from the relationship, I find that I am being
more helpful" (Gibb's italics). Then he lists a number of "role-
free" attributes—fourteen of them—indicating his closeness,
his genuineness, his humanness, his "freedom from planned or
habitual strategy" ("spontaneity"), and his freedom from "distancing" role responsibilities other than those of "being here,
now" *with* the other *person*.

His description, inadequately summarized here, suggests Goffman's (1961) ironic comparison of "sacred" and "profane" aspects of individual conduct, the latter part "attributed to the obligatory world of social roles . . . formal, stiff, and dead . . . [as] exacted by society." And, he continues, "The sacred part has to do with 'personal' matters and 'personal' relationships—with what an individual is 'really' like underneath it all when he relaxes and breaks through to those in his presence" (Goffman, 1961, p. 152). Goffman considers this a "vulgar" distinction, a "touching tendency to keep the world safe from sociology" (p. 152). One has "role distance," in Goffman's view, when one fails to "embrace" a "situated role." But the picture is complicated by equal opportunity to show "distance" from "non-situated" as well as "situated" roles. For Goffman, then, the concept of "role distance" is important in that it may shed light on personal style, however distance is manifested.

In the case of Jack Gibb's "role-free" person, I want to ask, Is the counselor or his client "role free" when he is unable to manifest "distance" from the situational demands of "role freeness"? For instance, is occasional irony, humor, or other less reverent attention to "what you or I are doing here," any the less "role free" than tears or touching or leaving the room to wash one's hands? When is "genuineness" genuine or "inner reality" real? I confess to obtuseness about "role freedom," but I am willing to grant that the concept is an important one for Jack Gibb and his clients.

The Problem of the Non-TORI

In conclusion, there is an even more vexing problem which Jack Gibb's prescription of TORI-ness poses for me. It can be stated in this way. Consider the WHIG, for example. He is not, as some might think, the member of an archaic political party. Rather, Jack Gibb has singled him out, by implication, as troubled (or trouble?) because he is not a proper member of any organization. Untreated, he abounds in human society. He is, again by implication, characterized by the undesirable personality traits of Withholding, Hiding, Impotence, and Gregariouslessness. That is why he may be called a WHIG.

Consider the TORI. He is not, as some might believe, a British conservative. Rather, by implication, he is the model member of whatever organization he belongs to. Once upon a time he, too, was an untreated WHIG, but now he is TORI, which stands for Trust, Openness, Realization, and Interdependence. Although his kind does not yet abound in human society, it will. Secure in that belief, the TORI is strong and confident. He is also generous—and that is the nice part of what can be told here—for the gift of love, earlier bestowed upon him, is now freely bestowed upon others. Since the TORI has been enabled to establish quick intimacy, even with strangers, his loving acts can be warmly received by others. By open invitation of this sort the TORI ranks are swelled. Under TORI leadership, again by implication, a new day of enlightenment is dawning for all mankind.

Compare the world of WHIG and TORI with that of Cincinnatus C., who lives in a "world of souls transparent to one another" (Nabokov, 1959, p. 24) and where for many years he, "comprehending his danger, carefully managed to conceal a certain peculiarity. He was impervious to the rays of others, and therefore produced when off his guard a bizarre impression as of a lone dark object . . . [for] actually Cincinnatus was opaque" (*ibid.*). A young man now, Cincinnatus C. has finally been exposed for his anomaly, arrested, tried, and convicted of criminal deviance. At some imminent date, unspecified, he is to be beheaded. One infers that Cincinnatus would not want to be transparent, even if he could. His terror is real, though, and he does not want to die.

Suppose that in a nation full of TORIs there were but one WHIG who did not want to change? Would he be treated like Cincinnatus? Are he and Cincinnatus to be considered less "role free" than their fellows? I wonder, Dr. Gibb. I wonder.

References

Goffman, E. *Encounters, Two Studies in the Sociology of Interaction.* Indianapolis: Bobbs-Merrill, 1961.

Nabokov, V. *Invitation to a Beheading.* New York: Putnam, 1959.

Stegner, P. *The Edge.* New York: Dial Press, 1967.

The Encounter

The primary difficulty encountered by the readers of Gibb's paper was gaining a clear picture of what was meant by being "role free." Pepinsky, in his paper, attempted to show that Gibb has prescribed a role—a particular way of behaving in the relationship even if it were to be "role free." This was extended in the discussion by Bach when he suggested that perhaps the rule system guiding Gibb was to "break rules." Nevertheless, the major problem of understanding precisely what was meant by such terms as "being personal" or "free" remained. Therefore, the elucidation of the meaning of behaving freely became the main focus of the discussion. Gibb related several examples of his behavior in groups which clarified his meaning. These have been included within their context in an attempt to make his meaning more clear.

MODERATOR: Dr. Pepinsky, you are not inclined to refute Gibb's theory. This is perhaps wise because, as you admit, and many of us agree, you don't have a full comprehension of the theory. What concerns us is the position you take, that it works *for Jack Gibb*. Does that mean that it wouldn't work for you? In my acquaintance with you I found you to be a warm, open outgoing person, certainly a person with integrity. Does this mean it won't work for you?

PEPINSKY: When I wrote this paper, I was asking questions. There are two ways to ask questions about what comes next. One question we can ask is, How do we institutionalize this sort of thing? But the other, and for me more important, question is, How do we avoid institutionalizing this process? A part of what you are responding to in Gibb's paper is that it is a very interesting exposition of how this can be set up and in effect how the next person can be invited to mass-produce it. I have to say I don't understand (in commonsense terms) the paper very well. If I have to report on the paper as one who knows Jack and one who has talked with him about what he is doing in California, then I understand it in a different way.

What I responded to in the paper, in a nonderogatory sense, was Jack Gibb's high level of artisanship, which has been revealed again at the conference in his capacity to make himself understood by me. As an old friend, I have to say, "Jack, when it comes to the written word, it didn't come through in the same way it does in conversation in watching you perform in groups."

There are things we can talk about here, but I don't want to pretend that either one of us is making sense out of this; I don't think we have to. I am probably somewhat responsible for suggesting that a counselor ought to be a theoretician, have a theory, but whether he ought to be expected to play by the same rules as someone who is trying to understand the process and trying to put it in the public domain—I am not at all sure we ought to expect that they be one and the same person.

GIBB: I think I am willing to talk about it either way. Very clearly for me, the thing I'm talking about is a way of living that "turns me on," that makes me more of a person, that satisfies my life and I feel is successful with people that I work with. I feel good about the groups I work with, and some research indicates that changes do occur.

So it is my personal preference to behave this way in the counseling situation, particularly in groups, where I feel the most effective counseling, by all odds, goes on.

I would be glad to engage in a dialogue on the second point. I think I can specify what it means to be relatively role free or to be personal in the counseling relationship. This can be learned and one can use the same kind of research tools for evaluating its effectiveness as he can any other specifiable mode of behavior.

Because it may not be very clear, let me try to say simply what I do in a counseling situation. I intend to come into the situation without any formal theoretical expectations of how I'll behave. I try to "hang loose." I don't bring in a plan or a strategy. I attempt to relate to the situation as impulsively, personally, and directly as I can. I don't intend to teach, to train, to help, to counsel. I intend to be as much a person as I can be. I intend to learn, to have fun, to confront people, to build a relationship. I intend to fight, to love. I intend to be there and behave and act with everything I can do. Incidentally, I believe that being this way satisfies the role obligations I have as a counselor or therapist in the situation.

One of the evidences this is so is that people who meet me after four or five years think I have changed a great deal. I'm still pretty timid; I'm threatened by all of *this*. I'm still not the spontaneous, free, easy, "turned-on" kind of person I'd like to be, but I'm much more so. I'm more comfortable with people, I'm more able to be present. I guess *available* is the critical word.

PEPINSKY: Well, when I first knew you, you were at the height of being your grim, rigid, methodological self. This is what I think is really fantastic.

GIBB: That is not as charitable a description as I would make [*laughter*], but there is no gainsaying the validity of your remark. I see myself that same way.

PEPINSKY: You were writing a book on methodology, and it was a very depersonalized book. You were intensely involved then, as you are now in a different way, in expressing ideas about how *things* work. You were interested in theory.

GIBB: I am still interested in theory, though less in things. I would rule out nothing in the counseling situation that the counselor can bring to it. In the relationship, if I had any insights about the client that he could understand, I would share them at whatever depth I was able to communicate them. I wouldn't hold back my interpretations, or my feelings, or my rejections, or my angers. I would reveal them as much as I was able to make them available. What would hold me back is my own fear and timidity. But I'm finding these fears are illusory —I can make available any behavior I am capable of and it is helpful.

An illustration would probably be helpful. A group of industrial executives started out. There were fifteen of us in a small group. It was a little tense. Some had been ordered to be there by their bosses. Something came up in the first half-hour and someone asked, "What were you feeling?" I said, "Well, what I'm feeling is very threatened by you, Joe. The idea of having to spend six days here with you in this group is depressing me. You seem like a very hostile kind of guy that does a lot of stuff that annoys me. I think, 'My God, if I have to be here six days, I want to leave.' " This was very hard for me to say, because it is not the kind of thing I normally say in a situation, but it was as close to how I felt right then as I could come. This threatened him and everybody. They thought, "What are we going to have to put up with with this kind of guy?" We went on to something else. About ten minutes later, this man turned to me and said, "That was essentially the same thing my boss said to me about a month ago, and what I'd like to look at is why people get these impressions of me." Then we were off. . . .

The point is that I'm learning not to inhibit the feelings that I have at the moment. I don't put them through a filter of "Will this be helpful?" "Is this person the particular kind of person for whom confrontation would not be therapeutic?" I don't ask these questions any more.

PEPINSKY: As I listen to this, it is much more down to earth than the language in your paper. If I were your student, I would find it extremely important to listen to you very carefully.

Why is it that the language used by the people at Bethel, who were doing their work very well, was such a difficult language to the outsider? There is quite honestly a language barrier. When you talk this way now, you come through; when you talk on the printed page, I have to read between the lines.

As you talk now you are being more concrete and illustrative. The language is a simpler language, a commonsense language that we are used to exchanging with each other. If I hadn't known you at all except through your paper, I would have said, "Gee, this person is practiced in the norms of evasion. Every term he uses, if I didn't know him, could be construed to be skillfully removed far enough from the events so that he is safe in talking about anything." When you say a counselor is role free, I'd like you to tell us more about that because the idea that comes to my mind is not what you intend it to be. One of the tasks for somebody, perhaps not you, is to make sense out of what is happening by starting at a more basic level of language.

GIBB: One of the things I mean by taking a role is that one takes on a strategy or stance or acts like Carl Rogers, or acts like Eric Berne, or he takes it upon himself to be a *helper*. "My role in this situation is that I'm the *helper*; I'm trying to help this other person to learn." Or I'm a teacher, or a parent. By these roles I prescribe what I'm supposed to do.

On the other hand, I come into the situation intending to be personal. I come in with whatever I am and I am going to be with another person for that moment. We interact, we relate, we communicate, we talk. One of the very significant findings that Lorraine and I have been experiencing for the last couple of years is the great importance of expressive coping behavior— hugging, touching, putting your arm around someone, smiling, holding hands, fighting, and all the rest of the things people do bodily and facially with all of the nonverbal behavior.

One of the things we have experimented with is to have a group session for two or three hours in which nobody can talk. When all talking is ruled out, people try to communicate with gestures, with a variety of things. This is a very amazing thing once people talk about it and learn how they bodily communicate warmth, anger, and other feelings in relationships with other people.

I walked into a marathon group at Esalen about two weeks ago during the night. They were meeting for twenty-four hours straight through the night, trying to be personal. They were pretty tired and pretty alienated. One person had been attacked quite a little by the group. He had received a lot of negative feedback and was hurt. People mentioned these events, and he looked as if he was hurt. As I walked in, I was a little threatened by the situation and what I saw as the demands on me. "What can I do in this kind of group? It is so threatening, people are so anxious and so angry." I began to talk a bit. Finally, somebody said, "This guy is hurting; what are you going to do about that?" He looked hurt about that time. So I said, "I feel really hurt by you; it make me feel compassionate and I'm all torn up by this. I feel like walking over toward you." I walked over toward him and held my arms out. He stood up and met me about a quarter of the way, put his arms around me; I put my arms around him. He put his head on my shoulder, broke down, and started to cry. I started to cry. I held him like a little boy for maybe thirty seconds or a minute.

Then a girl sitting next to him, who, in the first few minutes, had seemed to me to be quite frightened, broke down and fell

into our arms (we were sitting down on the floor by this time).
She started to cry and said, "How can you do that to him? How
can you walk up to a complete stranger and you and he cry, and
break down and feel all this compassion?" It was obvious to her
that here was a real person working with another real person,
having some compassion about each other's hurts. This communicated much better than words how I felt about him.

PEPINSKY: Jack, have you ever had the experience of
meeting somebody like this on the street two days later?

GIBB: Yes, I met a fellow at the Seattle airport who had
been in a group like that. Both of us walked up and put our arms
around each other much like the Russians. I didn't kiss him on
the lips but I did grab him and I held him for a moment. We
looked at and talked with each other for a few moments. I felt
great and he felt great. I don't know how he felt about people
observing but I thought it was tremendous.

This is what I mean by being impulsive and trying to do what
you feel like doing. I wasn't walking over to him to teach him
that people can be compassionate. I felt that way! Three years
ago I wouldn't have been able to do that. I would have been too
frightened. I would have wondered what he would think. As we
talked about it, he had a lot of concerns about that. I think it
was my realness and my impulsiveness, my genuineness that
helped him. He said that he couldn't remember ever being
hugged by a man before. His father hadn't done it. And it was
a very moving experience for him. *And for me.*

Now, if I say, "I'm going to behave like Gibb, because Gibb
walked into a group and that looked like a great gimmick—
you walk up to somebody and put your arms around him and
that establishes that you are authentically a real person" that's
nonsense. For me, in that moment, that felt good. It meant a
great step in growth in me and it was a great experience for me
regardless of what happened in the group.

3

Fact and Choice in Counseling and Counselor Education: A Cognitive Viewpoint

LEON H. LEVY
Indiana University

This paper is an attempt to describe how counseling and counselor education are conceptualized from a cognitive viewpoint. However, "cognitive" can mean many things since there is no single theoretical system which can be taken as either the origin or the referent for this viewpoint. Consequently it is necessary to state at the outset that the orientation represented by this paper is but one of many which might fall under the rubric of "cognitive." It draws heavily upon the ideas of George A. Kelly, as contained in his *Psychology of Personal Constructs* (1955), but departs from them in a number of ways which will be apparent in due course. The position I have taken is still evolving, far from full maturity, but it has already proved its serviceability in the teaching and practice of counseling and psychotherapy, and this is the justification for presenting it at this time.

Rationale for a Cognitive Approach to Counseling

Whether we look at counseling from the client's point of view or the counselor's, fact and choice emerge as basic elements. True, there may be disagreement between client and counselor on the nature of the facts and choices involved, but there generally is consensus on the notion that in the process of counseling facts will have to be determined and, ultimately, choices will have to be made. The counselor is expected to help the client consider all the facts, distinguishing between relevant and irrelevant facts, accept them, and make the most of his life in the face of these facts. Choices, which are expected to be the client's, are supposed to be based upon the facts. Thus Hadley (1958) has depicted the counseling psychologist as "most concerned with promoting the client's *objective* understanding of the current and present situation" (italics added). Although much has been written about counseling's goal of maximizing the client's development and freedom, inevitably this comes down to enabling clients to make better and more informed choices (Tyler, 1961).

Toward this end we engage in the measurement of vocational interests, aptitudes, and personality variables, so that these may be used by the client and his counselor in plotting the client's future course in life. Energies are expended and papers written on the compilation of occupational information files—again so that the client may have the facts he needs. Texts on counseling devote one or more chapters to the uses of tests and other sources of information in the counseling interview. The general notion is that if we create the right kind of atmosphere, i.e., one that is unthreatening, accepting, and warm, the client will be more receptive to the facts of his life and be guided by them in the decisions which he must make. This all seems intuitively plausible, and no doubt with a modicum of ingenuity we could even construct one or more counseling analogue experiments to enhance its plausibility.

However, the position of this paper is that the problem in counseling lies at another level. The problem in counseling, for both counselor and client, is in their conceptions of the nature of fact and choice. The prevailing view of anything labeled a fact is that it is existentially real, immutable, and indifferent to man. This is especially the case if a fact is called "objective," which, in the conventional rhetoric, usually enjoys the company of the adjectives "cold" and "hard." The implication is that the only appropriate posture in the presence of a fact is either acceptance or resignation. As both conventional wisdom and psychoanalytic dogma have taught us, only anguish can be expected when facts are denied or distorted. The time seems ripe to challenge this conception of fact and offer counseling the choice of a different one—one which promises to liberate both the counselor and his client from the tyranny of facts implicit in the conventional view.

Choice and decision have always been recognized sources of distress, frequently ending in uneasy compromises even when all the facts are known. But in this year of 1967 AD (after dissonance) no one would be so naïve as to expect that decisions once made are over with. Regardless of the alternative chosen, according to Festinger (1957) there is bound to be some residual attraction in the unchosen alternative and the grounds upon which it might have been chosen, so that some dissonance is expected to ensue from any important decision. Thus we are able to live comfortably with our decisions only by carefully sifting or distorting information which might increase this post-decision dissonance. Once again, the assumption is made that "the facts speak for themselves"—if we let them.

But there is the further assumption in this idea of choice that man abhors inconsistency and that therefore inconsistency must be either pathognomonic or pathogenic. This view of inconsistency is so common that it hardly needs documentation and its questioning may indeed seem supererogatory. Festinger (1957) grants dissonance status as an aversive drive on the order of hunger and thirst; a major portion of Rogers' theory of personality and psychotherapy (1959) rests upon the same concept; and a few years ago dissonance was proposed as the major source of motivation in a theory of career decision making (Hilton, 1962). Dissonance has also been postulated as the effective agent in mediating changes in behavior as a consequence of psychological interpretation (Levy, 1963).

Progress, however, rests largely upon our ability to question the unquestioned, and it may be time to reopen the question of the nature of choice and of dissonance. In particular, it may be profitable to question two of the major implications of these views: (1) that dissonance enjoys factual status, i.e., that, given knowledge of the facts of the person's beliefs, values, actions, and existence, the presence or absence of dissonance can be objectively ascertained, and (2) that in the best of all possible worlds everything would be consistent with everything else, i.e., that the reduction of dissonance is an understandable motive in the client and a legitimate problem for the counselor. How well supported are these implications? What are the consequences of rejecting them and the premises upon which they rest?

There are urgent reasons for believing that a different conception of facts and choice, and of dissonance, is necessary. They have to do with the changing intellectual climate of psychology and with the nature of the counseling process and counselor education.

The Changing Intellectual Climate of Psychology—To examine the changing intellectual climate of psychology first, consider the following:

1. Theories of learning and behavior have moved increasingly toward the postulation of mediational processes and away from explanations in terms of overt, physical stimulus-and-response variables. That is, they have moved toward a cognitive approach to the explanation of behavior. Hebb (1960) has called this the next step in the American revolution in psychology which began with the advent of behaviorism. It is well illustrated by three quotations, from a learning theorist, a developmental psychologist, and a clinical psychologist, respectively:

". . . we react more to our symbolic representation of things than to the things per se . . ." (Lawrence, 1963, p. 189).

"Man reacts less to the objective quality of external stimuli than he does to categorizations of those stimuli" (Kagan, 1967, p. 132).

". . . the facts of life take shape only as we plot them within the framework of a construction system, and the dimensions of that construction system are always subject to revision" (Kelly, 1955, p. 211).

Although these views are current, they are far from being new to psychology, as any reader of Lewin, Tolman, or Brunswick would testify. They have been standard fare in psychology's continuing debate over questions of the nature of the stimulus and what is learned. But they are now being taken seriously by the Establishment, and this is new. They are neither a rejection of empiricism nor a denial of an external reality. Instead, they are an argument for a more complex notion of man's interaction with his environment, one which sees man as an information-processing system whose behavior is to be understood in terms of the characteristics of that system. They represent a rejection of a *naïve realism* in which it was believed that the job of science is to *uncover* the laws of nature heretofore merely hidden from our view, and in which psychology attempted to build its laws of behavior exclusively upon the dimensions of observable events. They represent a recognition of the principle that to either understand, predict, or modify the behavior of an individual in a situation it is necessary to know the meaning of that situation to him. To know the facts of a person's existence, that is, we must first know the ways in which he codes his experience.

2. The scientific explanatory value of dissonance and of dissonance theory is being challenged, and it seems just possible that dissonance may go the way of homeostasis as an explanatory principle; it explains so much that its explains nothing. For example, while Brown (1965) grants that inconsistency may have general importance in understanding attitude change, he also notes that dissonance theory lacks the rigorous logical structure we require of a scientific theory. As a result, true tests of the theory are impossible, and, Brown suggests, the experiments performed in its name "only confirm the imaginative powers of a group of investigators" (p. 602). And Chapanis and Chapanis (1964), after a searching critique of research in cognitive dissonance, ask whether it is "really possible to reduce the essentials of a complex social situation to just two phrases" (p. 21). This is the essence of Festinger's definition of cognitive dissonance, and their answer is no. If these views are correct, perhaps it is time to look anew at the presumed consequences of inconsistency and choice.

3. There is, in fact, a growing body of opinion that inconsistency may not be inherently aversive or pathognomonic. Here we may note that Tiedeman (1967), in his recent presidential address to Division 17, argued strongly for the need of counsel-

ing psychologists to distinguish between *predicaments* and *problems*. Predicaments are to be lived with; problems are to be solved. The choice and pursuit of goals involves the person in the logically contradictory stances of tentativeness *and* commitment and of reflection *and* implementation, which Tiedeman defines as predicaments. To be fully human, Tiedeman maintains, the person must develop the capacity to tolerate both of these predicaments. To the extent that the counselor sees the predicaments as problems to be solved, he is preventing the person from gaining awareness of their existence and from realizing their value in his growth and development as a human being. Thus, while Tiedeman recognizes that inconsistency may be unpleasant, he also argues that in certain instances it may be an unpleasantness which counselors must help people learn to endure rather than eliminate, if they are to gain full maturity as human beings.

Evidence supporting a more positive view of inconsistency also comes from a study recently reported by Katz and Zigler (1967) of self-image disparity among fifth-, eighth-, and eleventh-grade children. Using measures of perception of real-self, ideal-self, and social-self, these investigators found that self-image disparity was positively related to chronological age and intelligence. The higher the developmental level of the child, the larger the inconsistency between his various self-images. Katz and Zigler propose that "Rather than being ominous in nature, increasing self-image disparity would invariably appear to accompany the attainment of higher levels of development, since the greater cognitive differentiation found at such levels must invariably lead to a greater capacity for self-derogation, guilt, and anxiety" (p. 194). Katz and Zigler recognize that their findings do not necessarily conflict with the large body of evidence relating self-image disparity to maladjustment, but they argue that before this disparity is given a negative interpretation in any particular case attention should be paid to possible developmental factors. In some instances, then, inconsistency may reflect growth rather than pathology.

Gergen (1968), in a provocative essay entitled "Personal Consistency and the Presentation of Self," suggests that the aversiveness of personal inconsistency, which is taken as universal, may in large part be a product of the demands and values of society and social scientists rather than a reflection of the intrinsic psychological nature of the individual. Consistency has become the ethic of the behavioral sciences, he argues, and, in the best traditions of the self-fulfilling prophecy, they have created the conditions which provide the evidence to support their position. But Gergen adduces sufficient evidence and arguments to support his suggestion that "the prevalent view that the normal behavior of individuals tends toward consistency is misconceived." He concludes, very much in agreement with Tiedeman's argument, with the question "Might it not be better to teach acceptance of the paradoxical, than to require as a 'mark of maturity' that the individual hang his identity on a limited set of his capacities for being?"

Thus a number of treasured truths in psychology are being challenged, the situation is fluid, and consequently we have one of the necessary conditions for further growth—if we take advantage of it. Fact and choice may still be important elements in counseling, but their status and our approach to them seem open to negotiation.

Counseling and Counselor Education—A number of considerations concerning the nature of counseling and counselor education also suggest that a reformulation of our conception of fact and choice may be desirable. They are actually presuppositions, and no attempt will be made to document them.

Clients wind up in counseling because, for one reason or another, they find that their own resources, and others upon which they may have called, have failed them. This failure may have been in connection with making a major decision, choosing a vocation, getting acceptable grades, getting along with others, or being happy with themselves. We may see some as oversocialized, some as undersocialized, some as dependent, and some as confused. It makes little difference. The point is that the facts, as they know them, have not helped; they may even have hurt. They have failed to make the grade, as students, as parents, or as persons, and have found their way to counseling.

It seems reasonable to assume that the client comes into

counseling because he has run out of alternatives. He can no longer count on himself alone to carry him through. He may or may not be anxious in the clinical sense, but he is immobilized. He is out of the race, at least temporarily.

Thus what the client needs from counseling, whether he puts it in so many words or not, is additional alternatives which he can try out, and assistance in becoming better able to cope with future stresses and problems. He needs to be helped to gain the resources to generate alternatives and choose between them in the future. Most importantly, he needs to learn a new stance in relation to his experience, a different perspective so that he can find his way out of the box he is in. Warmth and empathy, although important in creating the setting in which these needs can be met, may be cold comfort unless they are accompanied by new inputs directed to the needs themselves.

In a very real sense, many clients may be said to be the victims of naïve realism. The meanings of events seem all too fixed and all too ominous to them. True, in some instances we can point to neglected or distorted facts which seem responsible for the client's problem, but I suspect that these are only a minority of cases. Thus it is not additional information that is required as often as it is additional ways of interpreting information and better ways of "going beyond the information given" (Bruner, 1957).

In this situation the counselor equipped with a cognitive orientation toward behavior and personality would seem ideally prepared to offer help. The nature of this help will be described in more detail later. For the moment it is sufficient to point out that within this orientation, particularly in the form which it has taken in Kelly's (1955) personal construct theory, the counselor is less likely to fall into the same traps as his client; he is more likely to be able to take a different view of the world from the one his client has; and hence he is better able to provide the new and different inputs necessary to help his client move forward. Before he accepts his client's view that he has been rendered helpless by circumstances, he will consider the alternative that circumstances have been rendered helpless by his client.

Above all, in his training the counselor needs a model of man which will help him make sense of his client's behavior and of his own as counselor. Ideally, this model should not require him to shift his intellectual or scientific standards as he moves from one course to another in his training or as he moves from his training to practice. The behavior which he engages in as a student, which he observes in the scientist, and which he encounters in his client should be understandable to the counselor within the same theoretical model. He has to see his client, above all, as another human being, and his problems as continuous with all problems faced by man. The counseling situation then becomes but another instance of man attempting to cope with the conditions of his existence, and the counselor is less likely to see his client as sick, inadequate, or inferior. Counseling turns into another exercise in problem solving and creativity. It becomes educational rather than remedial or clinical, and each new problem is approached with venturesomeness and optimism rather than timidity and fear of what might be uncovered.

If the counselor sees the world as his client does, he has little to offer him. If the counselor subscribes to a naïve realism, all he may have to give in many cases is tea and sympathy. And one does not have to wait long to find the counselor emerging from an interview with a client and telling his colleagues or supervisor that he has to agree with the client, he is in an impossible situation, or he too would feel inferior if he were the client. The counselor has accepted his client's construction of reality and is thereby caught in the same iron grip of facts as his client. When all of the facts are in and the distortions cleared up, the counselor finds that he has joined his client in the same box. He too is immobilized.

But if the counselor has adopted a cognitive view of behavior and personality, he sees his client's problem as the result of how he has coded or construed events. He sees the solution to his client's problem in helping him find different ways of construing these events. He recognizes facts as constructions of reality rather than reality itself; if he finds that he can see only the same facts as his client, he takes this as meaning that they are both construing events in the same way, not that there is no other way of construing them. In this case the counselor's conceptual ability, audacity, and creativity are challenged, for he realizes

that the only way out for both him and his client is in their
ability to find a different and better construction of the events
of the client's life.

Fragments of a Cognitive Theory of Counseling

Does a cognitive approach to counseling do more than tell
the counselor to pay attention to how his client thinks? Does
it say more than that better lives depend upon better thoughts?
Does it provide the counselor with a model by which he can
understand his client's behavior and respond effectively? These
are among the most crucial questions that can be asked about
this approach. To provide the grounds for unequivocal answers
would require more space than is available here. In truth, it
would also require a more comprehensive and coherent theory
than is now available. But it may be possible to give tentative
answers on the basis of a number of conceptual fragments out
of which such a theory may eventually be fashioned.

Personal Constructs—Postman (1953) has stated that the
defining characteristic of a cognitive theory of behavior is its
attempt to explain regularities of behavior in terms of how the
organism discriminates and categorizes its environment. Kelly
(1955) has suggested the unit of analysis which might be applied in such a theory: the personal construct. Each person is
assumed to evolve a system of personal constructs by means of
which he structures his experience and anticipates events. These
constructs are dichotomous and arranged in a hierarchical system
so that they bear certain inferential relationships to each other.
In Kelly's view, behavior is largely governed by expectancies. As
he puts it in his Fundamental Postulate: "A person's processes
are psychologically channelized by the ways in which he anticipates events" (p. 46). By an analysis of the structure of an
individual's system of personal constructs—the kinds of constructs used as well as their number and ordinal relations with
each other—Kelly maintains that it is possible to account for
his behavior and his experience.

In effect what Kelly has done in his psychology of personal
constructs is to treat each person as though he were a scientist

who has evolved his own personal theory by means of which he interprets his experience. In this we may see similarities to the views of Heider (1958) and others who have proposed that an individual's social perception and interpersonal relations may be understood in terms of his implicit personality theory. The virtue of Kelly's approach, however, is in its elaboration of the various characteristics of personal constructs, including a method of assessing them, and in its emphasis upon the roles played by personal constructs in defining the alternatives a person sees open to him and the facts which emerge from his encounter with events. For counseling it becomes evident from the theory that we must first learn the constructs used by the client before we can determine how to help him. Ultimately, behavioral modification and help depend upon changes in the kinds of constructs used, the number used, and how they are used.

In this approach to counseling, it should be noted, the emphasis is not upon correcting faulty or irrational beliefs or illogical thinking, as is the case in Ellis' rational-emotive psychotherapy (1958). Constructs are either useful or not useful to an individual; their particular ordering, the kinds of inferences they lead to, is either helpful or not in his attempt to plot his course through life; the number of dimensions he uses may be too few to permit him sufficient flexibility of response in certain situations. These are the kinds of considerations which the counselor following this model keeps in mind in working with his client. Thus it is not rationality that the counselor is after in helping his client, but a better conceptual schema.

Personal construct systems evolve so as to help the person anticipate events. If he finds himself trapped by the facts, if he has run out of alternatives, it is because of the way he has construed events. The point of personal construct theory is that what is taken as fact and what are considered possible alternatives are entirely dependent upon the individual's system of personal constructs. In effect, the structure of his construct system determines the structure of his experience. But personal construct repertoires, like scientific theories, are also responsive to validating and invalidating evidence. Thus the counselor, by explicating the constructs his client has been using, by bringing into juxtaposition events which had previously been separated in his client's thinking, by the kind of experience he provides his client through his relationship with him in counseling, helps the client re-evaluate his constructs, try out new orderings among them, and possibly expand his construct repertoire. And as construct repertoires change, so changes behavior.

The means for doing all this are many and run the gamut from free association to role-playing and from providing normative information to psychological interpretation. They depend upon the client, his problem, and the setting. But regardless of the methods used, the guiding premise is the same. The aim is not gaining insight into unconscious motives and mechanisms or forcing the person into some predetermined mold which the counselor believes healthy or desirable. The client is responsible for his own life and his choices; the counselor is there to help him explore new ways of construing them.

Belief Systems—If personal constructs are thought of as the dimensions in terms of which the person discriminates and categorizes his environment, it would seem necessary to provide for the stored product of their application beyond the immediate situation. It is not clear that Kelly has done so. That is, the person stores up the content of his experience over time, and any comprehensive cognitive approach to counseling should presumably deal with it as well. The most prominent example of such content in present-day thinking in counseling is undoubtedly the self-concept. But there are surely other beliefs which enter into the final equation determining the individual's perception and behavior. Together, they represent what Rokeach (1960) has called the individual's belief system and Tolman (1952) labeled "belief-value matrices." Although it may be true that the contents of belief systems are intimately associated with individual systems of personal constructs, probably something is gained by treating belief systems as separate components of the person's cognitive structure. As such, they would be seen to account, most immediately, for the choices and directions taken in individual behavior. Beliefs and values, then, are formed along the dimensions provided by personal constructs but provide an additional means of understanding the individual from a cognitive standpoint.

Rokeach (1960) has shown that the nature of an individual's belief system, whether it is open or closed, and the relations between his belief and disbelief subsystems enter not only into his social attitudes and behaviors but also into his general cognitive functioning. The counselor may turn to the belief system as a way of assessing his client's construct repertoire, as a means of understanding his client's actions, or as another source of leverage in moving his client off dead center. In focusing upon the belief system the counselor will of course be intimately concerned with his client's self-concept. But he will see it as just one of many components of the total belief system and will be led to consider his client's beliefs about society, work, and authority, among other things. These too may be important in particular cases. In working with an individual client the counselor will also become sensitive to the contribution made to his client's beliefs and expectancies by the counseling relationship itself, and his approach will be at once more complex and more flexible as he becomes aware of the specific beliefs which seem responsible for his client's difficulties.

If the counselor has had a reasonable grounding in the philosophy of science, which all psychologists should have, he will recognize that the activity he and his client are engaged in is no different from that of the scientist and theorist. They are examining various formulations and hypotheses in order to find the best fit between them and the phenomena of the client's life. The nature of the activity and its rationale are the same; only its scale differs.

Mechanism of Change—The mechanism of change in this approach to counseling is through changes in the nature of the client's construct repertoire and the contents of his belief system. Feelings, needs, and motives are not ignored, but they are viewed as part of the context in which solutions are to be sought and as subject to reconstruction themselves. As construct repertoires change and possibly increase in complexity, new pathways of movement open up, alternatives shift in meaning and may increase in number, the very questions and problems posed may change, and new facts emerge from the person's experience. For one client the world became less bleak when he came to see that some of his behaviors and feelings which he had feared were symptomatic of homosexuality were better construed as a desire for love and affection, some as an expression of a fear of rejection by women, and some as the result of circumstances which had little to do with his personality or sexuality. Another client found he could make peace with his father after he was able to see him as neurotic and insecure rather than a bastard and competitor. A coed, who was well above average in intelligence but on the verge of flunking out, began to improve her grades when she concluded that being a brain and being lovable were not antithetical. And another client discovered that his career choice was considerably easier after the grounds for it shifted from whether he should or should not satisfy his parents to considerations of his own personal growth and gratification. Thus, changes in the inferential relationships between constructs and the introduction of new constructs bring changes in the structure and meaning of the context in which solutions are to be sought and in the nature of the problems themselves. In like manner, alterations in belief systems bring about alterations in what the person believes possible and impossible, true and false, acceptable and unacceptable, and ultimately in what he will do.

These various cognitive changes are not regarded as insights. Most uses of this concept derive from the psychoanalytical mold of thought in which insight is equated with the discovery of Truth, heretofore nestled away somewhere in the Unconscious. From a scientific standpoint the concept, used in this fashion, is meaningless because there is no way of ever confirming or disconfirming the truth value of insights. From a therapeutic and social psychological standpoint the concept has some unfortunate implications. For example, it casts the therapist or counselor in the role of authority or seer since he invariably makes the final judgment concerning the truth value of the insight. In practice, the client has gained "insight" when his construction of events agrees with his therapist's (Levy, 1963). This means that the counselor can never be wrong, or that the client can never disagree with his counselor and be correct. Where insight is a highly valued commodity, the client is led to focus more upon its attainment as his goal in counseling than upon changes in his behavior and life situation.

The cognitive changes in counseling are no different, in essence, from those wrought in a scientific theory. In both instances a set of phenomena must be accounted for, and in both instances there is no means of determining whether a particular accounting is the true one in any absolute sense. We can only judge how comprehensive, logically consistent, productive, and useful any cognitive product is, whether it derives from a counseling interview or a scientific investigation.

Choice and Dissonance—By now it should be apparent how facts are regarded by the counselor working within the particular cognitive orientation described in this paper. It is neither a case of advocating that thinking will make it so nor one of accentuating the positive. It is simply taking the same view of them at the level of the individual in counseling as we adopt at the level of scientific investigation: The meanings of facts are functions of the cognitive structures in which they are embedded; and the function of cognitive structures, as of scientific theories, is to provide a stable, coherent, and usable interpretation of events. A bit more should be said, however, about choice and dissonance. Choice rests upon information and cognition, but it is also a potential source of information and cognitive growth. The choice of an individual reflects his learning, and his learning reflects his choices. Thus, choice may be viewed as a bridge between the person's past and his future, as a station on his path to maturity. Through his choices he tests the adequacy of his constructs and beliefs and exposes himself to the events out of which these may continue to evolve.

But if dissonance theory held in any rigorous sense, this would not be the case. Having made a choice, the theory asserts, we avoid any information which might be inconsistent with the choice; we seek only to confirm the course we have chosen. It argues, in effect, that we seek only redundant information. Hence, choice should not result in growth, except by accident, according to any strict reading of dissonance theory.

However, while there is more than a kernel of truth in the theory, its message for counseling might be read somewhat differently. That is, it might be taken to be describing how a client may be expected to act if he construes dissonance as valueless and responds only to its aversive quality. But if the notion that consistency represents the ideal in nature is abandoned, perhaps clients can be helped to make better use of dissonance and tolerate it better.

Although it may be overstating things a bit to say, as F. Scott Fitzgerald did, that the test of a good mind is the ability to hold two contradictory thoughts at the same time, the inability to do so may very well be the measure of a simple one. The point is that, if a client were helped to construe dissonance as a reflection of sensitivity to the complexity of nature and of most important decision situations, he would be less likely to close his eyes to the values represented by his unchosen alternatives and the information supporting them. In consequence, he would be expected to grow in cognitive complexity, to become less categorical and dogmatic in his thinking, and would thereby become increasingly able to cope with the complexity of events. He would no longer be looking for simple answers, nor would he need them.

Movement from the Categorical to the Contingent—In the final analysis, the benefits of this movement from what may be termed a *categorical* mode of thinking to a *contingent* one should go beyond the problem of choice and ultimately redound to the person's acceptance of himself and of others. The categorical mode, which is usually accompanied by either-or thinking, is marked by the client's assumption that there is a perfect consistency in nature such that he may take the form and content of a sample of a person's behavior as sufficient basis for judging or labeling him as an entity. It is entirely response-oriented in its view of man, taking no consideration of the conditions under which different behaviors are observed and thereby failing to appreciate the actual variability in behavior and the degree of its contingency upon particular events. This mode of thinking is most strikingly evident in the fears of homosexuality brought into counseling by many college students. Thinking categorically, they treat homosexuality as an entity. Believing that one either is or is not a homosexual, and having engaged in some homosexual act or having had strong feelings of attraction toward another male, they fear that they are *a homosexual*.

In helping such a student move toward a contingent mode

LEON H. LEVY 73

of thinking the counselor would attempt to get him first to apply his construct of homosexuality to his behaviors and feelings rather than to himself. Then he would explore with the client the circumstances under which these behaviors and feelings occurred, searching out the contingencies that might account for them. In some instances this would lead to changes in his perception of his behaviors and feelings—they would no longer be "homosexual"—while in others the client would come to recognize that they occur only under certain circumstances. In either event, in shifting toward a contingent mode of thinking the client would no longer view his feelings and behaviors (or those of others) in a diffuse and global fashion but would achieve a better understanding of them and more control over them. Thus, the counselor, in helping his client shift from a categorical mode of thought toward a contingent one (which in Kelly's system would represent a shift from constellatory constructs to propositional ones, and which, much earlier, Lewin had defined as Aristotelian and Galilean approaches to scientific explanations, respectively), is helping him move from a view of his world as fixed and absolute in its meanings toward one in which it is fluid and responsive to his participation.

The Experiential Component of Counseling—A word should be said about the role of the counseling relationship within this orientation. Clearly, the quality of the counseling relationship must have an effect upon the outcome of counseling, whether it be cognitively oriented or otherwise. But from a cognitive standpoint the relationship represents only the medium through which client and counselor communicate with each other; the focus is upon the content of this communication rather than upon the medium. To be sure, there is a sense in which McLuhan's (1965) currently fashionable epigram, *the medium is the message,* is true in counseling, but it is unlikely to be all of the message by a long shot. The counseling relationship itself may indeed provide the client with some information, particularly about the validity of his beliefs concerning interpersonal relations, but it would be grossly inefficient if we failed to make use of man's symbolic processes and relied solely upon the experiential component of the counseling relationship in trying to communicate with clients and modify their cognitive structures. From a cognitive standpoint the counselor would be concerned with establishing what has been generally accepted as a therapeutically beneficial relationship, but the extent to which he depended upon the relationship as the agent of change in counseling would be in inverse proportion to his estimate of his client's ability to profit from the cognitive component of verbal communication.

At the same time it should be noted that nothing in this view precludes the use of direct suggestion, recommendations, and advice. These may be used in two ways. For all of the reconstruction which might occur within the counseling session, the final test of counseling's adequacy must be in the marketplace. Unless a client who now sees his fear of dating girls in a new light actually makes dates with girls, or the client who has learned to distinguish between disagreement and aggression is able to check this out by disagreeing with his instructor or a fraternity brother, it is doubtful that these cognitive changes will ever reap the therapeutic benefits expected of them. While some clients spontaneously translate their cognitive gains in counseling into action outside of it, some need additional encouragement to do so. From a reinforcement theory standpoint, of course, this is simply giving the client positive reinforcement for desired behaviors and beliefs. From a cognitive viewpoint, it is a means of providing the client with feedback on the appropriateness of his behaviors and beliefs. Thus suggestions and recommendations are considered supplementary, rather than alternatives, to the cognitive inputs provided by the counselor during counseling sessions.

This principle applies in another sense also. That is, there are certain concepts and beliefs which resist adequate symbolization and which can probably be dealt with only experientially. For these the cognitive theorist may use graded tasks or specific recommendations in order to provide the necessary experience. Moreover, there are obviously certain social skills which depend largely upon practice for their perfection. Counseling may well set the stage so that the client can benefit from such practice, but ultimately the client will have to engage in the practice to realize the benefit. Suggesting to the socially immature college student that he attend a student government meeting, and later that he join a square dancing group, and still later that he try his luck at round dancing, need not be ruled out by a cognitive theory of counseling; after all, we don't live in our heads all the time.

The point which should emerge from the foregoing comments on the use of the relationship and of suggestion, advice, and recommendations is that the conception of counseling informed by the theory just sketched out is pluralistic rather than monolithic. It is more pragmatic than it is dogmatic; although it seeks to explain the counseling process in cognitive terms, it gives wide scope to how these may be implemented. It is built upon the same premise that we seek to communicate to the client, one which Kelly (1955) has very descriptively called "constructive alternativism."

Cognition and Behavior: A Model—Cognitive theorists have long been accused of leaving the organism "buried in thought" (Guthrie, 1952). Therefore it may be appropriate to indicate in a general way how the individual's beliefs and constructs may be expressed in overt behavior. For this purpose the conceptual model proposed by Miller, Galanter, and Pribram (1960) seems most promising. According to it, behavior is organized and controlled by a feedback arrangement in which all behaviors and situations are tested for congruence with the organism's Images and Plans. The Image represents the organism's values and beliefs, its stored knowledge of its environment, while Plans are those strategies or sequences of actions which the organism has established for achieving its goals and coping with its environment. Neither Plans nor Images need be conscious, and the concept of Plan is extended by these authors to include even primitive reflexes, which may be conceived of as governed by built-in sets of plans. They propose that behavior is controlled by a sequence of steps beginning with a test for congruence with the organism's Images and Plans. If the steps are found congruent, the behavior occurs or the organism's situation is accepted as is; it exists, and the sequence ends. If found incongruent, they are operated upon and tested for congruency again. This sequence of testing and operating continues until congruence is achieved and the element exists from the sequence.

Although the model is admittedly schematic, its value lies in its offering a plausible way of conceptualizing the counseling process from a cognitive standpoint. That is, by equating the client's belief system and personal construct repertoire with the model's Images and Plans, one may see how alteration in the client's cognition can bring about changes in his behavior. While plausibility is certainly no substitute for research and verification, where knowledge is limited, it is a necessary condition for the concerted action out of which knowledge may grow. And this is no less the case in counseling than in any other human endeavor.

We are not saying that a cognitive interpretation of the process of counseling is wholly without experimental laboratory support. Several lines of research might be mentioned as particularly relevant. Schachter and Singer (1962) have shown that identical states of epinephrine-induced autonomic arousal may be described quite differently by naïve subjects depending upon the kinds of cognitive inputs available. If subjects were experiencing the physiological effects of increased autonomic activity in the presence of an experimental confederate who was clowning around, they interpreted their experience as a pleasant one; if the confederate, on the other hand, suggested that they were being put upon by the experimenter, the subjects reported their experience as one arousing anger or resentment. Thus, the quality of affective experience appears to be dependent upon cognition. The same conclusion might be fairly drawn from the work of Lazarus (1966) and his associates, in which it has been shown that the presence or absence of stress in response to a potentially threatening stimulus depends upon the subject's cognitive appraisal of the stimulus. Here subjects viewing a film of a primitive subincision ritual demonstrated relatively little stress if they construed the film as an interesting anthropological document. Although in the psychoanalytic canon this would be interpreted as intellectualization, it may be alternatively construed as an example of the role of cognitive dimensions in the appraisal of threat. Lastly, mention might be made of the growing body of research involving the role of cognitive complexity in personality impression formation (Crockett, 1965) and in decision making (Schroder, Driver and Streufert, 1967). This research shows that quite different impressions and judgments emerge from the same pool of available information depending upon the nature of the constructs used by the person and their interrelationships. Taken as a group, the different lines of research suggest that to the extent that counseling is able to modify a client's cognitive structure it should be able to modify his view of himself and the world about him. By helping the client develop a new cosmology, as Hobbs (1962) has put it, the counselor is helping him find new ways to interpret and order his experience. The task remains of verifying this within the context of counseling.

Implications for Programs in Counselor Education

The demands placed upon a training program intent upon producing counselors prepared to function within the cognitive orientation just presented are extensive and not easily met. They cannot be satisfied in a direct fashion solely by courses in techniques of counseling, occupational information, the uses of tests in diagnosis, and professional problems. Valuable as such subjects may be, they become secondary in producing a counselor with the philosophical and intellectual orientation required by this approach. Most importantly, course content alone will not provide the counselor with the personal security essential in one who would part company with the conventional, the obvious, and the approved in order to open himself to new experience and growth. In this approach, as in the client centered, the counselor functions as both agent and model (Berenson and Carkhuff, 1967) in his client's reconstruction of his life. However, there are fewer prescriptions of how he operates than there are in client-centered counseling, so it is likely to be the more personally demanding of the two, particularly with respect to his ability to make full use of the freedoms and alternatives open to him.

Milieu—It is thus apparent that one of the major parts of a counselor education program never appears in college catalogues as either an elective or a required course. For one thing, while

this program obviously entails the acquisition of certain specialized knowledge, it also entails the acquisition of particular attitudes toward this knowledge. More important, it entails personal
development in the broadest sense of the term. And the latter
depends upon the intellectual and emotional milieu of the program, the experiences of the student in formal courses and in
his practicum supervision, and the examples set by his instructors and supervisors. Where dogmatism reigns, whether it be
in the name of client-centered empathy, reinforcement theory,
or cognitive theory, all that can be hoped for are technicians and
caricatures. As everyone is well aware, a great deal of learning
occurs through identification and modeling—particularly in the
realm of values and attitudes. Thus, the graduates of a counseling
program will be no more imaginative, flexible, and open to new
experience than their instructors; and clients will be no more
imaginative, flexible, and open to new experience than their
counselors.

This does not mean that viewpoints should not be presented
with enthusiasm and commitment. It does mean that there
should be equal enthusiasm and commitment to the principle
of open inquiry and exposure to alternative viewpoints. It does
not mean that we must either tolerate or foster muddled thinking; a good part of what counselors have to offer their clients is
a way of thinking, one which is clear as well as imaginative. It
does mean that we must take care not to force premature closure
in the realm of ideas, for it is in his own training, first of all, that
the counselor must learn how to divine the hidden assumptions
of thoughts, how to explore the consequences of different assumptions, and how to impart a certain adventurousness and
excitement to his client in groping for better solutions to his
problems. This ability can come about only through a training
program which itself is exciting and daring, with the emphasis
more on discovery and exploration than on the learning of cate-
chisms and methods, and with respect for the student not solely
contingent upon his mastery of course content and conformity
to some particular party line. There would appear to be considerable merit in our heeding McLuhan's (1965) observation,
"We are entering the new age of education that is programmed
for discovery rather than instruction" (p. ix). Therefore, we have

every reason to agree with Patterson's (1964) observation that the conditions which lead to student growth are essentially similar to those which have been postulated as necessary for client growth.

The implication is that developing a counselor education program calls for as much attention to the quality of its milieu as to its curriculum. Although this is certainly not a new observation to counselor education, the nature of the milieu suggested may be new. However, the milieu will carry us just so far in the training of a counselor, so it is now necessary to consider briefly questions of curriculum.

Curriculum—Only those aspects of the curriculum which may be distinctive or particularly important to this approach will be discussed. They also help to shape the program's milieu, of course, but in addition they provide the counselor with the wherewithal to profit by this milieu and to practice his profession.

Course content. As noted earlier, a sound grounding in the philosophy of science is of special value in improving the counselor's understanding of the viewpoint represented here. This may be gained either in a separate course or from courses primarily devoted to theories and systems in psychology. Although the student will be engaged in a helping profession, familiarity with the tenets of the philosophy of science will make him appreciate the continuity between the character of the help he offers and the activities of the scientist. Moreover, this instruction may also cause him to better evaluate the scientific validity of the concepts he applies and immunize him against the not uncommon confusion found in counseling between metaphysical and scientific propositions.

Of obvious importance in providing the counselor with the theoretical foundation for his practices are courses in the psychology of learning and cognition. The curriculum also achieves its distinctive character in a strong emphasis upon social psychology, particularly in the areas of communication and persuasion, attitude change, role theory, and social perception. These are exceptionally valuable for understanding the nature of the counseling process. It is becoming increasingly clear that the counseling relationship has much in common with other interpersonal situations, and consequently the field of counseling would seem to have much to gain from the findings of researchers working with these other kinds of social situations. The recent book by Goldstein, Heller, and Sechrest (1966) is illustrative of the rich mine of material awaiting the counseling psychologist with sufficient ingenuity to familiarize himself with these areas of research.

Practicum. The counseling practicum—pivotal, of course, in any training program—is here viewed as a laboratory in human behavior as well as a workshop for the forging of future counselors. Although most students enter practicum with the expectation of learning the practical side of counseling—how to interview, how to "reflect feeling," how to help—an effort is made to get them to see it also as an opportunity to learn more about human behavior. This is essential for their own development as well as for the profession's since it will be a long time before we can point to an established body of theory as the foundation for our practices. In supervision, therefore, as much time (or more) is devoted to discussing the client's cognitive structure and how it may account for his present behavior and problem as is spent on questions of technique. Supervision is somewhat less concerned with the student's knowing what to say, when, and how, than with his learning how to analyze behavior and understand its cognitive underpinnings.

Thus the supervisor is cast in the role more of collaborator than of fountain of wisdom; he is more a co-investigator than a preceptor. He proposes interpretations and hypotheses for the student to consider and invites the student to do likewise. Through listening to tapes and going over interview notes and test data with his supervisor, the student learns how to listen to his clients so as to distill the major constructs and beliefs by which they have structured their lives. Supervisory discussions center around the inferential relationships between the client's constructs and his belief systems, what alternatives the client sees before him, and what changes in the client's cognitions would be most desirable and practicable. Technique is surely discussed, but it is secondary to understanding.

Inevitably, through his practicum experience the student becomes more aware of his own constructs and belief systems, and
often they undergo change and growth as a consequence. But
this is never the intent of supervisory conferences. The focus is
always on the client unless the student shifts it to himself.
Nevertheless, it must be recognized that for the student the
supervisory conference shares many of the characteristics of
the counseling interview, particularly as he discusses some of his
frustrations and confusions in dealing with his client. Thus a
certain amount of incidental learning is expected to accrue
from these conferences: the student comes to know how it feels
to be a client, and the supervisor provides him with a model
for his role as counselor. In this way the student has an opportunity to observe good counseling practice in action and also to
experience its effects. Given a good supervisory relationship, it
would be hard to imagine a better arrangement for learning
good counseling practice.

A concern which is not uncommon among students beginning their training is what happens in counseling if they make
an error—if they interpret when they should be accepting, are
passive when they should be active, make the wrong interpretation, and so forth. This kind of concern reflects the student's
belief that for each client remark there is but one perfect counselor response. It is fostered by supervisory sessions which take
the form of Monday-morning quarterbacking. Unfortunately,
there is probably nothing more hobbling in counseling than
such an attitude. At the very least it means that the student is
paying more attention to himself than to his client, and it certainly means that he is unlikely to confront his client with the
spontaneity, genuineness, and openness which is essential to effective counseling. If there is one critical problem in practicum
training, this is it.

The problem can be overcome to some degree by counting on
the incidental learning which occurs during supervision for a
major share of the student's training in counseling techniques.
It seems just possible that this is the best way for the techniques to be acquired. That is, behavior learned through identification or modeling seems more likely to come out in counsel-

ing as the student's own, spontaneously and appropriately, than
behavior which has been prescribed or learned solely through
explicit instruction.

But concern about technique and mistakes can be further
reduced if the student is helped to see the counseling process
within a cognitive framework in which there is a constant inter-
play between behavior and knowledge. If the counseling relationship is fundamentally sound, the transactions which occur
within it tend to be essentially cumulative and self-corrective,
not too different from those which occur in scientific inquiry.
This point is of great importance in counselor training for it
means that errors of omission and commission are seen by the
student as eventually corrected over the course of the counseling
relationship, and they are less likely to be regarded in absolute
terms or as disastrous in their consequences. The student therefore becomes somewhat less apprehensive as he confronts his
client and is in a better position to learn from his errors at the
same time that he learns how to avoid them. The result is that
the practicum becomes a genuine laboratory in human behavior
at both theoretical and practical levels.

The foregoing view of practicum and the counseling process
in no way implies a lessened concern with the welfare of the
client or respect for him as an individual. It does mean that
something more than the desire to help is expected of the student in counseling. Unless this desire is also accompanied by a
desire to learn and to produce new knowledge, and unless both
desires are fostered by instructors, we shall probably be training
students only in the perpetuation of the obsolete.

References

Berenson, B. G., and Carkhuff, R. R. *Sources of Gain in
        Counseling and Psychotherapy*. New York: Holt, Rine-
        hart & Winston, 1967.

Brown, R. *Social Psychology*. New York: Free Press, 1965.

Bruner, J. Going beyond the information given. In *Contemporary
        Approaches to Cognition*. Cambridge, Mass.: Harvard
        University Press, 1957. Pp. 41–69.

Chapanis, Natalia P., and Chapanis, A. Cognitive dissonance: Five years later. *Psychological Bulletin*, 1964, *61*, 1–22.

Crockett, W. H. Cognitive complexity and impression formation. In B. A. Maher (ed.), *Progress in Experimental Personality Research*, Vol. 2. New York: Academic Press, 1965. Pp. 47–90.

Ellis, A. Rational psychotherapy. *Journal of General Psychology*, 1958, *59*, 35–49.

Festinger, L. A *Theory of Cognitive Dissonance*. New York: Harper & Row, 1957.

Gergen, K. J. Personal consistency and the presentation of self. In C. Gordon and K. J. Gergen (eds.), *The Self in Social Interaction*, Vol. 1. New York: Wiley, 1968.

Goldstein, A. P., Heller, K., and Sechrest, L. B. *Psychotherapy and the Psychology of Behavior Change*. New York: Wiley, 1966.

Guthrie, E. R. *The Psychology of Learning* (rev. ed.). New York: Harper & Row, 1952.

Hadley, J. M. *Clinical and Counseling Psychology*. New York: Knopf, 1958.

Hebb, D. O. The American revolution. *American Psychologist*, 1960, *15*, 735–745.

Heider, F. *The Psychology of Interpersonal Relations*. New York: Wiley, 1958.

Hilton, T. L. Career decision-making. *Journal of Counseling Psychology*, 1962, *9*, 291–298.

Hobbs, N. Sources of gain in psychotherapy. *American Psychologist*, 1962, *17*, 19–34.

Kagan, J. On the need for relativism. *American Psychologist*, 1967, *22*, 131–142.

Katz, Phyllis, and Zigler, E. Self-image disparity: A developmental approach. *Journal of Personality and Social Psychology*, 1967, *5*, 186–195.

Kelly, G. A. *The Psychology of Personal Constructs*. New York: Norton, 1955. 2 vols.

Lawrence, D. H. The nature of a stimulus: Some relationships between learning and perception. In S. Koch (ed.),

Psychology: A Study of a Science, Vol. 5. New York: McGraw-Hill, 1963. Pp. 179–212.

Lazarus, R. S   *Psychological Stress and the Coping Process*. New York: McGraw-Hill, 1966.

Levy, L. H.   *Psychological Interpretation*. New York: Holt, Rinehart & Winston, 1963.

McLuhan, M.   *Understanding Media: The Extensions of Man*. New York: McGraw-Hill, 1965. Paperback ed.

Miller, G. A., Galanter, E., and Pribram, K. H.   *Plans and the Structure of Behavior*. New York: Holt, 1960.

Patterson, C. H.   Supervising students in the counseling practicum. *Journal of Counseling Psychology*, 1964, *11*, 47–53.

Postman, L.   Perception, motivation, and behavior. *Journal of Personality*, 1953, *22*, 17–31.

Rogers, C. R.   A theory of therapy, personality, and interpersonal relationships, as developed in the client-centered framework. In S. Koch (ed.), *Psychology: A Study of a Science*, Vol. 3. New York: McGraw-Hill, 1959. Pp. 184–256.

Rokeach, M.   *The Open and Closed Mind*. New York: Basic Books, 1960.

Schachter, S., and Singer, J.   Cognitive, social, and physiological determinants of emotional state. *Psychological Review*, 1962, *69*, 379–399.

Schroder, H. M., Driver, M. J., and Streufert, S.   *Human information processing*. New York: Holt, Rinehart & Winston, 1967.

Tiedeman, D. V.   Predicament, problem, and psychology: The case for paradox in life and counseling psychology. *Journal of Counseling Psychology*, 1967, *14*, 1–8.

Tolman, E. C.   A psychological model. In T. Parsons and E. A. Shils (eds.), *Toward a General Theory of Action*. Cambridge, Mass.: Harvard University Press, 1952. Pp. 279–361.

Tyler, Leona E.   *The Work of the Counselor*. New York: Appleton-Century-Crofts, 1961.

Is Cognition Sufficient?

C. H. PATTERSON
University of Illinois

The paper by Dr. Levy presenting a cognitive viewpoint in counseling created in me a state of cognitive dissonance. The viewpoint is inconsistent with my theory and approach to counseling. And since I abhor inconsistency (which I do not believe must be pathognomic or pathogenic), I must do something about it. There must be some way of reconciling (apparent) differences between honest and intelligent individuals; after all, neither can be wrong.

But *was* it cognitive dissonance that I experienced, or was it affect arousal? Is cognitive dissonance entirely cognitive, or is it always associated with, or followed by, affect? Is man a rational being, or is he essentially a rationalizing being, using reason in the service of affect and emotion? Are choices and decisions essentially rational, based upon logical analysis of the problem and alternative solutions, or are choices and decisions influenced by feelings and emotions? Are psychological problems the same as scientific problems, to be solved through logical analysis?

The answers to these questions should be obvious. At least they are to me, although I do not claim to be a completely rational being and admit to rationalizing. It would seem to me obvious that counseling is not a rational, logical process, or the application of rational, logical procedures with a client and his problems. Nevertheless, this is a widely held concept, at any rate among a certain segment of counselors. Perhaps—and this may be a new insight to me—it is this concept of counseling which leads to the insistence on differentiating between counseling and psychotherapy. But if counseling is differentiated from psychotherapy on the basis of being a process of rational problem solving and decision making—or, as Weitz (1964) proposes, developing problem-solving skill—then it becomes difficult if not impossible to differentiate counseling from teaching, or individual tutoring. If counseling is not psychotherapy, is counseling then not teaching? It appears that the concept of counseling as a cognitive or rational process is prevalent among academically oriented counselors and counselor educators, including the University counseling center staff, and counselor educators whose background is in education, with little or no psychology. Levy seems to accept this concept of counseling when he says that counseling becomes "another exercise in problem solving and creativity. It becomes educational rather than remedial or clinical. . . ." What about the client who requires no education, or even re-education, but needs to find out who he is, what the meaning of life is or could be for him, how to reduce the discrepancy between what he is and what he wants to be or can be, how to get rid of crippling feelings and attitudes?

It is, of course, true that cognition is receiving increasing attention. Perhaps it has, in the recent past, been underemphasized in the study of behavior and in education. But, in the characteristic manner of human beings, the pendulum may be swinging too far in this direction. Some counselors may be so sensitive to trends and so fearful of being left behind that, to mix a metaphor, they are jumping on the pendulum and being swung into outer space.

Now, of course, psychologists, as scientists, claim to be rational and objective. But it is interesting to note the affective strength with which this claim is defended. I have been impressed, incidentally and parenthetically, with the *feeling* with which editorial reviewers of psychological journals condemn an author for showing *his* feelings and values.

The neocognitivists, to coin a word, have the new look. That is, they recognize the influence of perception (which has affective elements) on cognition, and Levy makes it clear that "the facts" are not the objective facts sought by Sergeant Friday. His is not a "naïve realism" but actually a phenomenological viewpoint: "to either understand, predict, or modify the behavior of an individual in a situation it is necessary to know the meaning of that situation to him. To know the facts of a person's existence, that is, we must first know the ways in which he codes his experience." Facts do not, then, exist in some external world or constitute an external reality; they are constructed, or created, by the individual. Facts are the perceptions, concepts, meanings, attitudes, constructs, beliefs, etc., held by the individual. This is a phenomenological position. If one understands that "fact," as used by Levy in his description of the counseling process, is the meaning of the situation to the client, one can accept, at least in part, his statement that "The counselor is expected to help the client consider all the facts, distinguishing between relevant and irrelevant facts, accept them, and make the most of life in the face of these facts." One might substitute "meanings" or "perceptions," then, for "facts." But when one does that, it becomes apparent that the statement does not describe all of counseling, since it is possible, and perhaps desirable, that meanings and perceptions should change as a result of counseling. Thus, counseling does not accept facts as immutable, to be accepted and adjusted to by the client.

Cognition and "Facts"

The question which arises when one uses the term "facts" in this way is whether counseling is, or can be, a purely cognitive process. To apply the term "fact" may give it the appearance of a cognitive process, but the definition of fact given by Levy suggests that it is only an appearance, based upon the use of a word associated with cognition but not, as defined, necessarily a purely cognitive term, as witness the cognates which are suggested: "meanings," "concepts," "perceptions," etc. Are such "facts," or perceptions or meanings, affect free, or rationally determined? The new "look" in perception, dating back to the study of Postman, Bruner, and McGinnies (1948) on personal values as selective factors in perception, makes it clear that perception is not a purely cognitive process but involves affect as well. Facts are not entirely objectively determined and thus cannot be treated as objective and impersonal, or apart from the emotions of the individual. Levy, of course, recognizes this.

Man is not a rational being, living in a "real" world of "facts." He is an affective, rationalizing being living in a phenomenological world which he in a sense creates and to which he gives meanings—and the meanings are influenced by his feelings and emotions. The fact of man's nonrationality is clearly demonstrated in his persistent claim to being rational in the face of the overwhelming evidence that he is not rational.*

The individual is a unitary organism, with cognitive, conative, and affective aspects, none of which can be divorced from each other and dealt with separately. Therefore, any approach to counseling or psychotherapy must recognize the affective nature of man.

This view, long accepted in education, is epitomized in the statements that the whole child comes to school and that teachers teach pupils, not subject matter. If the affective factors are important in subject matter learning, are they not more important in the learning which occurs in counseling or psychotherapy, with its infinitely greater ego involvement? The difference is belittled by those who attempt to emphasize the similarity of teaching and counseling. Representative of their attitude is the slogan that teaching and counseling are alike except that the subject matter of teaching consists of academic disciplines while the subject matter of counseling is the client himself, the implication being that this difference is not significant. I have sometimes suggested, perhaps minimizing similarities for the sake of emphasizing the differences, that the greatest similarity of counseling and teaching is that both make use of a fifty-minute hour.

There are, of course, similarities, since both deal with a total human being. Education recognizes the importance of the affective aspect of the person. Perhaps it may be contended that many approaches to counseling or psychotherapy do not adequately recognize the cognitive aspects. The difference between teaching and psychotherapy may be essentially one of emphasis, with teaching emphasizing cognitive learning while recognizing the influence of affective factors, and psychotherapy emphasizing affective change while recognizing cognitive factors. In the

* Nicholas Hobbs (Sources of gain in psychotherapy, *American Psychologist*, 1962, 17, 18–34), in discussing the strength of the belief in the efficiency of insight, relates it to "our strong general commitment to rationality in problem solving. As F. S. C. Northrop has pointed out, western culture (in spite of its immense irrationalities) has a deeply ingrained rational component. For us, reason is a faith. From earliest childhood we are taught to apply rational principles to the solution of many kinds of problems."

client with deep personal problems, however, affective factors overshadow cognitive factors, and the counselor must recognize and deal with these. Rational thinking and behavior may be a goal of counseling, but it may be that once the affective factors are dealt with the client will need little if any help in working through the cognitive aspects of his problems. Yet peculiarly Levy seems not to accept greater rationality as a goal of counseling: ". . . it is not rationality that the counselor is after in helping his client, but a better conceptual scheme." A rational approach to counseling or psychotherapy must be one which recognizes and deals with the affective and nonrational nature of man. Counselors must *feel* with their clients rather than *think* with them.

The importance of the atmosphere in counseling is its relationship to the affective aspects of the client's problem. A therapeutic atmosphere is anxiety reducing, desensitizing the client's emotional reactions to his experiences. It is nonthreatening, leading to self-exploration, or dealing with affect-laden, ego-involving ideas. Absence of threat, and the accompanying reduction of anxiety, has been demonstrated to lead to greater exploration and improved problem solving in noncounseling situations and to client self-exploration and therapeutic personality change in counseling (Truax 1963). Thus, Levy's statement that the client will be more receptive to the facts of his life and be guided by them in an unthreatening, accepting, and warm atmosphere, though intuitively plausible, but apparently not demonstrated, is simply not true.

The virtues of inconsistency seem to be overrated by Levy. If, as the aphorism says, consistency is the virtue of simple minds, then our greatest scientists have been simpletons. Inconsistencies certainly exist, and we must accept some, but the acceptance of all can lead to passivity. Refusal to accept inconsistencies is the source of discovery and scientific advancement. Levy misreads history if he feels that it is inconsistency which reflects growth. It is the refusal to accept inconsistency itself, and certainly not its acceptance, that results in growth. There is a need for consistency in human beings, perhaps constituting or including the need for self-consistency or the need for integration. The striving for consistency, the reduction of apparent contradictions, leads to the development of theories and systems which in turn spur investigations and experiments designed to test hypotheses of consistencies. In addition, while a moderate amount of inconsistency may constitute a challenge and lead to growth, great inconsistency may constitute a threat and lead to disturbance.

Interestingly, Levy presents a dualism in his approach to counseling. On the one hand, he points out that the client needs help because he has run out of alternatives, which the counselor must supply. Yet, at the same time, he states that "Most importantly, [the client] needs to learn a new stance in relation to his experience, a different perspective so that he can find his way out of the box he is in." Thus, it seems, it is not so much new knowledge as new perceptions which are necessary; counseling is not the suggestion of new alternatives by the counselor but the emerging of new alternatives in the client as a result of his new perceptions. Again, "it is not additional information that is required as often as it is additional ways of interpreting information." While Levy apparently considers this a highly cognitive process, it appears to be one involving feelings and emotions.

Counselor and Client

The problem of counseling or psychotherapy, then, is not getting the client to think differently but getting him to feel differently. In fact, it may be suggested that the *way* to get people to think differently is to get them to feel differently, and thus to perceive differently. One need only consider the different thinking of the depressed and the manic individual to recognize the influence of affect on perception and thinking. One does not try to change thinking in counseling, therefore, but to change feelings and perceptions. The achievement of this change is not by means of information giving, analysis of alternatives, teaching problem solving, or applying logic, but through providing a safe, secure, nonthreatening relationship in which self-exploration and changes in perception can occur. The counselor does not—indeed, cannot—change the facts or perceptions of the client. Only the client can do so. The counselor can facilitate—or hinder—the process, however. Intervention of the cognitive kind, I suggest, hinders rather than facilitates perceptual change. It may facilitate the solution of essentially cognitive problems, or assist in the making of choices in which affective factors are minimal. But this, it is proposed, is not counseling, but teaching, and probably not what most clients who need and want counseling require.

The cognitive approach apparently has little confidence in the client. The client cannot be depended on to solve his own problems or effect his own change. The providing of an atmosphere or conditions for client self-exploration and changes in perception is not considered sufficient. Levy states that "If the counselor sees the world as his client does, he has little to offer him." He must "provide the new and different inputs necessary to help his client move forward." Yet the counselor must see the "client's problem as the result of how he has coded or construed events," which Levy feels is a cognitive process. But this is empathic understanding, achieved by adopting the internal frame of reference of the client, and hardly a purely cognitive process. The solution to a client's problem is, as Levy notes, helping him find different ways of construing (or perceiving) events. But this is not achieved, except possibly on an intellectual or verbal level, by a cognitive approach. It is not verbalizations about the events which must change, but the perceptions of the events.

Again and again in counseling I have found that the client can and does change his perceptions—or his personal constructs —when the counselor enters his frame of reference and sees things as the client does. When a client says, "Things are completely black," the counselor may simply respond, "Everything is completely black." Then the client is enabled to say, "Well, perhaps not everything," or, "Well, perhaps not completely." But if the counselor responds by saying, "Things can't be completely black," or "Everything can't be completely black," the client will probably reiterate his statement or defend it, thus leading to resistance to changing his perception. I recently supervised a student who was working with a child. For several interviews the child reported incident after incident of being picked on, discriminated against, misunderstood, etc. The student counselor felt that no progress was being made, so we looked closely at what he was doing. It became apparent that he was not in the client's frame of reference but was seeing the child as being somewhat paranoid or showing ideas of reference. The client did not feel he was being understood or accepted and persisted in trying to get the counselor to see things as he did.

Now, seeing things as the client sees them does not mean, as Levy seems to say, that the counselor agrees with the client and accepts the client's perceptions as being unchangeable or not in need of change. On the other hand, it is not necessary for the counselor to keep reminding himself and the client that there is a difference between the client's perception and the counselor's, or that understanding of the client's perceptions does not mean acceptance of them as fixed. And it does appear to be sufficient that the counselor see how the client perceives things for the client to begin to change his perceptions. This is what empathic understanding is. The new perceptions are those of the client; he must change his perceptions. The counselor cannot offer or provide new perceptions, which are his own, and which cannot become those of anyone else. Kelly apparently recognizes this when he notes that the counselor does not attempt to pass his own constructs on to the client; if he should do so the client would translate and change them to fit his own construct system (Kelly, 1955, pp. 593–594).

Thus does Levy fuse concepts and percepts, reason and affect, logic and psychologic, and the behavior of the scientist with the process of developing personal constructs.

The scientist qua scientist is not functioning as an ordinary human being in relationship to his environment. Although he is not entirely able to shed his humanity to become an objective observer and analyzer, in the pursuit of science he strives to do so. That it is not a natural, ordinary, or easy thing is attested to by the difficulty, and incompleteness, with which it can be achieved. Therefore, the analogy of the development of the individual's personal construct system with the practice of the scientist is misleading. True objectivity would make of man an (almost) affectless human being. It would, or should, lead to more homogeneity and less conflict between the personal construct systems of individuals. Scientists also, if they were successful in achieving rationality, would evidence less disagreement (often accompanied by considerable feeling) than they do.

The difficulty seems to lie in not assigning affect the place it should have in the development of personal construct systems and in their change. Affect seems to be implicit in Kelly's system, certainly as an underlying factor in the rigidity and resistance to change of personal constructs. But peculiarly it is not recognized and dealt with, at least overtly and explicitly, in counseling. In the same way emotion seems to permeate personal constructs, which determine one's facts or one's perceptions, yet no overt recognition is given to the emotional component pervading the personal construct system. Personal constructs are said to be responsive to validating and invalidating evidence, but the resistance to such evidence indicates their emotional component. And it is, of course, known that one's hypotheses can be confirmed by manipulation of events and data in response to strong emotions or belief or desire to see certain results.

If there is one thing that experience and experiment in psychology has demonstrated, it is that attitudes, beliefs, perceptions (and personal constructs) are not altered easily if at all by logic, reason, and argument—that is, by rational approaches. Yet cognitive counseling proposes to do exactly this. To quote Levy, "the activity he [the counselor] and his client are engaged in is no different from that of the scientist and theorist." This activity, he says, leads to "changes in the nature of the client's construct repertoire and . . . belief system. Feelings, needs, and motives are not ignored, but they are viewed as part of the context in which solutions are to be sought and as subject to reconstruction themselves," presumably by the same cognitive approach. The resulting changes—indeed, all changes—are apparently regarded as cognitive changes. Yet they are not "insights," which are "equated with the discovery of Truth," but are simply alternative ways of construing or perceiving events.

It is interesting how strongly theorists resist the acceptance of the relationship as the effective element in counseling. They view it instead as the substratum, the nonspecific context, or, as Levy terms it, the medium. There is probably no doubt that what is added to the basic relationship has some influence on the outcome, but questions may be raised as to the necessity or desirability of this influence. However, if one defines counseling as teaching, as many, including Levy, apparently do, perhaps something more than the relationship must be provided, something of the kind Levy describes.

The statement that "it would be grossly inefficient if we

failed to make use of man's symbolic processes and relied solely
upon the experiential component of the counseling relationship
in trying to communicate with clients and modify their cognitive structures" needs some experimental support, particularly
when it has been pretty clearly demonstrated that the relationship alone does lead to change, and to change from more emotional to more rational behavior.

The Cognitive Counselor in Action

The difficulty with the cognitive approach as outlined by Levy
is not necessarily its goals, nor its description (at least in broad
outline) of the process of change in counseling. The goal of
counseling is change in perceptions or the personal construct
system, leading to changes in behavior. The counseling process
involves exploration by the client of new ways of perceiving or
construing events, choices, decisions, etc. The difficulty is the
methods by which change is induced, the techniques of counseling. Can change be achieved by the methods proposed by the
cognitivists, even when applied in a warm, nonthreatening relationship, if the latter can actually be provided using these
methods? The reason for doubt and questioning is that perceptions and personal constructs are not purely, or even mainly,
cognitive. It appears that Levy equates cognitions with perceptions or personal constructs. This equating is deceptive and lends
plausibility to his argument which it does not merit. The research
he cites provides evidence for the importance of perceptions,
with their affective components, rather than for cognition, which
is, or has always been, contrasted with affect.

If there is cause to believe that cognitive counseling is not
effective with emotional problems, how does one account for
the (apparent) success of the approach? The answer is relatively simple. Cognitive counselors do not do what they say
they do—or, perhaps better, they do not limit themselves to
cognitive counseling. They can and do offer a relationship.
Like the behavior therapists, they state that this is not the
effective element, but they have not demonstrated their claim.
Their effectiveness may be, and probably is (as with behavior
therapy) more the result of the relationship than added spe-

cific techniques. It is high time, especially in view of the evidence we have for the effectiveness of the relationship alone, that those who claim added effects from specific methods or techniques demonstrate the effects rather than assuming them. We cannot accept success as evidence for the effectiveness of the approach unless it is shown that the success is not or cannot be achieved by the relationship alone.

The implications for counselor education suggested by Levy do not appear to be closely related to the cognitive approach to counseling which he outlines. His methods are not highly cognitively oriented. There are no courses in logic, reasoning, pitfalls in thinking, argument and persuasion, or in social, cultural, educational, occupational, and other information, which should be very much part of the background of a cognitive counselor. There may be an overemphasis on learning and cognition as compared to personality and emotion. Few, if any, would disagree with the comments on the milieu of counselor education, however. The practicum, on the other hand, may seem to reflect the cognitive approach, with much time spent in "discussing the client's cognitive structure and how it may account for his present behavior." But if one reads "perceptual structure" or "personal construct system" for "cognitive structure," there would probably be little objection. It is interesting that Levy places little emphasis upon technique and specific interventions, whether in terms of analysis of the student's past interviews or with reference to what he should do in future interviews. "Technique is surely discussed, but it is secondary to understanding." There can be scant disagreement with the general discussion of supervision.

The foregoing discussion may be obscured by terminology. Levy uses the term "cognitive" in its generally accepted meaning as covering all aspects and means of knowing, including perceiving as well as recognizing, judging, reasoning, and conceiving. Difficulty and confusion arise, however, in that the view of the nature of perception has changed. Perception is no longer seen as being determined by, or isomorphic with, external stimuli or the excitation of sensory receptions. In other words, perception is not purely cognitive but has affective aspects or components, as well as conative elements. Thus the old classification of mental processes into cognitive, affective, or conative is no longer possible. All mental or psychological events or processes, and all behavior, as indicated earlier, partake of all three aspects. Levy includes affective elements in his cognitive approach through recognizing their influence on perception. His approach is accordingly not purely cognitive in the old sense of being separate from or excluding affect. His cognitive viewpoint is clearly not a solely intellectual or rational approach to counseling.

My criticism, therefore, is directed to the relative emphasis on a rational, logical, intellectual approach as compared to an emphasis on an affective, experiential, relationship approach to counseling. To me the former is an overemphasis on the non-affective aspects of psychological problems, or a lack of recognition of the affective influences on behavior. The question is not one of either-or, but of more or less. The difference, however, is not to be minimized. The emphasis in dealing with psychology and problems in counseling or psychotherapy should, in my opinion, be heavily on the affective, experiential side. The development of skill or effectiveness in this area should be the focus in counselor education. The stress on the rational and the logical in all other areas of education should be sufficient to assure that the cognitive (nonaffective) aspects of counseling will not be neglected. In fact, the greatest problem in counselor education, I believe, is getting counseling students to reduce the cognitive factor and attend to the affective aspects of the client, his problems, and the relationship.

References

Kelly, G. A. *The Psychology of Personal Constructs.* Vol. II, *Clinical Diagnosis and Psychotherapy.* New York: Norton, 1955.

Postman, L., Bruner, J. S., and McGinnies, E.   Personal values as selective factors in perception. *Journal of Abnormal and Social Psychology,* 1948, *43,* 142–154.

Truax, C. B.   Effective ingredients in psychotherapy: An approach to unraveling the patient-therapist interaction. *Journal of Counseling Psychology,* 1963, *10,* 256–264.

Weitz, H.   *Behavior Change Through Guidance.* New York: Wiley, 1964.

The Encounter

Two major themes were discussed at length. The first was the necessity for consistency, on the one hand, and the tolerance of ambiguity or paradox, on the other. Levy expanded the concepts of his paper to illustrate how a person must be able to live "conditionally" even though he operates within a consistent system of beliefs. What became rather clear in the discussion is Patterson's apparent belief that there is a universal set of laws upon which the universe is based and that science is concerned with the discovery of those laws.

The second theme developed the differences between the two men regarding the usefulness of cognition in counseling as opposed to or in conjunction with the relationship.

Levy touched on both themes in his opening remarks. Rather than present those remarks as he made them, we have introduced them as "leaders" into the two themes.

LEVY: So far as training students is concerned, beyond all else the student needs some frame of reference from which he can make sense out of the client's behavior and out of his own behavior. This might be one of the conventional personality theories or some strictures about just being yourself—but he needs a frame of reference. The approach I've outlined in my paper is the one I think would be most helpful.

Each person behaves according to a set of rules, strategies, or beliefs. This is not an unreasonable assumption. This view is gaining acceptance in many theories of learning, animal as well as human. The doctrine of "immaculate perception," as Abraham Kaplan referred to phenomenology, is untenable in the light of all we know of human behavior. We code all our experience and we act according to that code. We can help a person best by understanding the codes and the interrelations among them and helping him change them. This does not imply that, as Patterson seems to think I believe, the person is a completely rational person or that he acts on a set of syllogisms. We try to explain his behavior rationally but do not believe he is continually acting in a rational fashion nor do we try to argue him out of some set of beliefs that he has.

The rules, strategies, or beliefs we talk about are inferences made from the counselor's observations; we never get at the raw constructs just as we never get at the raw feelings. When a person talks about his feelings, he is, in fact, making inferences about them. Quite clearly the nature of the affective experience depends upon the cognitive input—what seems plausible to the person. When it comes to changing behavior, what we are concerned with is changing the person's cognitive structure—his belief system—the dimensions along which he sorts out his experiences.

PATTERSON: I begin with the assumption that there are no differences—that there is consistency or else science would be a meaningless endeavor. I assume Dr. Levy is an intelligent person and I like to think I am one also. Since we are two intelligent human beings, neither can be wrong. Therefore, there must be some form of agreement. The problem is to find the consistency. The same thing is true of the current controversy between behaviorism and relationship therapy. These are both facts; both work. If there is truth in both, there must be some way to reconcile them. This shows my need for consistency—perhaps I am alone in this—but there are others like me. Lecky's self-consistency theory would be an example.

Levy says everyone operates on a system. This shows that the individual is striving for consistency; when consistency breaks down he comes for counseling.

LEVY: I think it is true that clients come in when they experience some inconsistency. The question, for me, is whether we should attempt to resolve inconsistency in all instances or should help them live with some inconsistencies—those circumstances that existentialists would say are part of our human condition.

PATTERSON: Yes, there are such inconsistencies, just as there are anxieties one must learn to live with. But the counselor should attempt to reduce the inconsistency. In order to act, ambiguity and inconsistency must be resolved at least temporarily. They may build back up again, but action demands they be resolved.

LEVY: Yes, in effect you can't take action unless you have polarized your beliefs in some respect. For example, increasingly, we find students who are troubled by fears of homosexuality. This seems to be a growing concern and invariably it arises out of feelings they have or behaviors they have engaged in that don't fit in with their idea of the masculine, competent male—they have to be strong in all respects.

It seems to me that this fear comes about in part because we have elevated the notion of consistency to the point that, when they observe some inconsistency in their feelings or some ambivalence in their attitudes, they think, "My God, something is wrong someplace." I think the idea of love as the thing we are working toward may be unrealistic. I wonder if a person wouldn't be helped better—be more fully aware of himself—if he were able to recognize hatred as being human, as being a part of a person, as well as love.

That is what concerns me in what I regard as an overemphasis in striving toward consistency. Sometimes you are a conformist, sometimes you are not. Sometimes you're close to people, sometimes you're not.

MEMBER OF AUDIENCE: Could you relate this to the position Dave Tiedeman took in his paper?

LEVY: Yes, I alluded to this in my paper. In essence, I agree with him: There are some things that are irresolvable.

PATTERSON: The problem with that is that it could lead to an easy way out by labeling things predicaments rather than problems and then you don't have to do anything about them. If everything is a predicament, then I don't have to do anything about it—so why worry?

LEVY: This is a very real danger. If you adopt the position I'm advocating—that there are some inconsistencies you do have to learn to live with—it may become a rationalization, but we have to accept the fact that we are in a risky business.

VANCE: How is that different from the notion that all relationships are fraught with *ambivalence* and that we have contradictory feelings not only toward other persons but toward things in general? I'm trying to think why what you are saying is different from what one might read in an ordinary account of ambivalence. What is there in the cognitive theory or personal constructs that would see that differently from the way anyone in the field would?

LEVY: I'm not sure there is any real difference. I should say I don't think this is necessarily a part of either a personal construct or a cognitive approach. It is one thing that I personally feel is very important from my recent readings of existential psychotherapy.

VANCE: Do you encourage people to explore their inconsistencies and try to identify the predicaments?

LEVY: Well, yes, we encourage people to explore them and we explore them. We are very purposive in our approach to therapy. At times we feel we do not want to bring about change. We feel that the reason this person is hung up is because of certain attitudes he has, and the way to bring about change is to make him clearly aware of inconsistency.

VANCE: Let's take a homosexual. When you see that homosexuality is a concern, you automatically hope he will learn that bisexual orientation is part and parcel of human nature for all?

LEVY: Yes, if this is his worry. We have many different concerns about homosexuality. We try to move people from a categorical orientation to a conditional orientation. We ask, "Under what circumstances or conditions do you behave otherwise?"

At this point Dr. Vance expressed his interest in identifying the "real" differences in treatment approaches. To set the stage for the ensuing discussion, excerpts that appeared to be relevant were taken from the opening remarks of both Dr. Levy and Dr. Patterson.

LEVY: The counselor serves as both an agent of change and a model for change. In an informal discussion, Dr. Gibb stated that he doesn't believe that humans model others' behavior. There is a considerable body of research to support the notion that they do. Part of the counselor's task is to not accept the client's naïve realistic view of the world—that "these are the facts," that "this is the way it is." The counselor should be able to say, "This is one way of viewing the world, and these are the dimensions you are using." To the extent that the client can see that the counselor is able to find other ways of construing the same events, the client begins to model the counselor. The client now begins to search for alternate constructs of a set of events and he feels less trapped by those events.

The responsibility of the counselor includes changes in behavior as well as in cognition. We are not satisfied if the client just *thinks* differently. Sometimes this translation from cognition to behavior is just having the client feel less anxious, but to stop short of changes in behavior is not to do the job.

One of our students would not ask whether he has faith in his client, which apparently is very important in some systems. Rather, he would ask whether he has accuratey assessed his client's potentialities, both his assets and his liabilities. He would be more concerned with how he has perceived his client and vice versa. He would be concerned with how he has been *perceived* by his client rather than whether he has unconditionally accepted his client. I have trouble conceptualizing "unconditional acceptance" and I feel that it would not ever be a desirable thing to put into operation in any literal sense.

And finally, the notion that a cognitive approach is completely rational and that it denies emotion and feeling is an erroneous one. Emotion and feeling are not denied; they are very important in therapeutic concerns. But the kinds of feelings experienced are seen as dependent upon cognitions. The analogy between the client and the scientist performing experiments and testing hypotheses was not meant to portray the client as a "cold fish" devoid of feeling and emotion—that perception is based upon a false view of science. This is not meant to be a super-rational approach.

PATTERSON: I agree that changing a person means changing personal constructs. We may use different words, but we are all interested in changing a person's constructs.

It is true that present-day psychology doesn't separate cognition and perception. I tried to point this out in my paper. If that is true, then Dr. Levy is not dealing with cognition in the old sense, and his system is not a cognitive system, unless cognition is all of psychology.

LEVY: I wouldn't engage in a great deal of intervention or suggestion of alternatives early in therapy, and with some clients, never. I recently had a very disconcerting experience with a student who took everything I had said and everything Kelly had written literally and began in the first session to say, "Well, you have been looking at it this way. You could just as well call this sensitivity as something else!"

MEMBER OF AUDIENCE: What you just said indicates you start out to build a relationship and don't start with your intervention. What we have not done is to recognize adequately the interaction between affect and cognition. Man starts out basically as an affective being, age zero. He *becomes* a cognitive individual. It may be we can teach some things only after we have a certain kind of relationship.

PATTERSON: The question is not "Is the relationship necessary?" but "Is the relationship sufficient?" I think there is evidence that the relationship is sufficient for certain kinds of change—the kinds of change that are more affective in nature, the kinds of change that are not so cognitively oriented, that do not involve rational choices and decisions.

LEVY: I agree that one of the differences *is* whether we think relationship is sufficient. Obviously, I don't, although I think it is important. I think it is the medium through which we reach the client. I know of no study where relationship by itself has been a variable. There has not been a study where content has been held constant or made irrelevant to the client's problem.

Where you see the *relationship* as the effective variable, I am concerned with *why* it is the effective variable. I attempt to account for it in cognitive terms: "What has the person learned? What does the experience mean to him? How does he interpret this positive experience he has had?"

PATTERSON: I think the central issue is one of human relationships. That is the basic human problem that people come to counseling with, unless they come with a learning problem. You can make some broad distinctions. This is where diagnosis comes in. Within the realm of personal relationship problems, there is no point in trying to break this category into subcategories. Psychiatry has tried and failed. We ought to give up after several hundred years of trying and recognize that difficulty in human relationships is a unitary kind of problem. But there are other kinds of problems that people have—problems of learning—which require different approaches, and here the approach is teaching, not therapy.

MODERATOR: In your paper you say that "intervention of the cognitive kind . . . hinders rather than facilitates perceptual change." You suggest that cognitive inputs of any kind get in the way of perception. Do you mean to go that far?

PATTERSON: In the paper I am asking a question, but I believe that often the input of the counselor interferes with the personal constructs or cognitive structure of the client. I think changes have to come from him. It is the same thing with reversible images. The change is determined from within, and if you try to tell an individual how to see things, he doesn't. It interferes with his shifting.

LEVY: I can't see where cognitive inputs in the form of interpretation will hinder changes in perception. These inputs are occurring haphazardly in a person's everyday life. Why should it hinder if they occur more systematically in the course of counseling or psychotherapy? What we are doing by feeding new things into the system is simply giving the person more information to process, challenging the assumption he is making, stretching some of his constructs, helping him see that some of these are not adequate. As a result he shifts around and looks for others that are better.

PATTERSON: The client who comes for counseling already recognizes they are not adequate; he is already searching. You can facilitate the search and leave it up to him if you provide a nonthreatening relationship.

There is, however, another reason for avoiding interpretation. You agree with most people that interpretation is generalizing, abstracting. We have some evidence now, from the Truax studies, that concreteness is related to self-exploration and that it is desirable that the counselor be concrete rather than abstract. This seems to be another argument against interpretation.

LEVY: Not really. It is a matter of the rhetoric of interpretation. One of the most difficult things for a beginning student to learn is how to talk meaningfully to a client, particularly with respect to interpretation. I say, very often, that the language should be picturesque and dramatic in order to get through to clients. Useful interpretation is in terms of the person's concrete experience.

TRUAX: I agree with much of the cognitive approach,

probably because I like to think of myself as rational. But I wonder, if it were really true that your cognitive theory accounted for behavioral change, why would you bother seeing clients? It would seem much more sensible to prepare essays and brochures with alternative constructions spelled out. These could then be given to clients—even in a nonthreatening environment.

LEVY: You are confusing the conceptual, explanatory model with how one brings about change. Though we talk about a person's personal constructs, it isn't just a matter of providing him with alternative constructs, and it isn't a rational process. We very often engage in what we call loosening of the thought processes, engage in free associations, talking about dreams as a way of opening a person up so that he isn't so concerned with having everything fit into a nice logical system. Once he is able to forego some of the rigors of logic in his thinking, we can begin to introduce alternatives, or they occur to him.

TRUAX: That is my point. The cognitive model as presented here does not explain the motor force for change as you are now describing it. You are saying, "We have to go away from the cognitive model to talk about how we produce change."

LEVY: There are two things operating as far as a motor force for change is concerned. First of all, the person is unhappy; he is in some sort of distress. This doesn't mean he is willing to give up his cherished and lifelong beliefs. The therapist must help to loosen him up so that he can consider alternative ways of thinking about himself.

TRUAX: This seems to be the difference between you and Dr. Patterson. He is talking about relationship factors as conditions for inducing cognitive and other kinds of changes, whereas in your paper you are not dealing with what *produces* cognitive changes but only saying that cognitive changes have to occur.

LEVY: I suppose I didn't deal with that to any great extent. I did indicate that I thought the relationship was very important. The emphasis was on the cognitive conception of behavior, and I didn't get into precisely the techniques that are used to bring about change. But the therapist confronting the patient as a real person and not as a technician is very important if he expects the client to trust him and to have confidence in him. You may say that this isn't *cognitive,* but I have trouble drawing the line.

VANCE: I can now see that some of the difference is in the goals you would have as opposed to Dr. Patterson and Dr. Gibb. If I put the three of you on a continuum, the other two would be on one end wanting spontaneous, somewhat "thoughtless" behavior while you would be on the other end wanting clients to be thoughtful and reflective about their behavior in order to take considered action.

LEVY: No, I would want him to be thoughtful and considered *in therapy,* but when therapy is over, ideally, he wouldn't worry whether he is conforming or not conforming. He feels he is behaving as he should. But until you get to that point, you have to work through the beliefs and constructs a person has.

GIBB: I agree with the point that the *spontaneous, thoughtless stance* is more appealing to me. But a personal relationship is a full organic relationship in which a person reacts with his thoughts, his feelings, his attitudes as an integrated person in the relationship. I was asked to talk about an immediate intuitive position and I stressed that more because of the set of the paper. I certainly would not rule out thinking, perceptual change, or even arguing with the client. I would stress spontaneity and thoughtlessness more than I hear Dr. Levy doing.

BLOCHER: Dr. Levy, you expect that the client, after counseling, is much less constricted cognitively, much less self-conscious and rigid. Behaviorally he would appear very free and spontaneous.

LEVY: I would be very pleased with a client coming out that way.

4

The Psychological Interview as a Discovery Machine

FORREST L. VANCE
University of Rochester

Some of you, I suspect, are already angry with me. Besides, I mean, those of you who know me very well and therefore have good reason to be perturbed with me from time to time (and I with you, which is comforting evidence to a clinician that our underlying mutual affection is still alive and strong).

But what makes me think that some of the rest of you are already "obnoxed" (in the current adolescent idiom) by my presentation? Have I flipped my lid at last? Am I putting you on? Have I been overexposed to people who automatically dislike anyone over thirty? Or is there some plausibility to my expectation of an element of irritability in your reactions?

Let me list some things for you to be irritated about, so that, if you honestly cannot think of any on your own, I can help you to get at least a little worked up, in order to confirm my hypothesis:

1. I am making a speech at you. This is not a procedure that I conceive to be a source of rapturous fulfillment for you (or for me either, I might add).

2. I have not yet established, and may never establish, that it is more appropriate that I talk and you listen than vice versa.

3. Most important of all, the title of my presentation is irritating in at least three ways:

a. The choice of the word "psychological" to characterize the interview process, as opposed to "clinical," "therapeutic," "counseling," or what have you, may well strike you as bigoted, arrogant, or stupid.

b. The word "machine" suggests a mechanical and insensitive approach to interviewing.

c. The title as a whole smacks of a kind of distressing flippancy concerning a serious topic.

If you are still with me, we have now completed a major portion of a working model of the kind of process I wish to explore with you. I want to examine the process of formulating and testing clinical hypotheses and to compare it with the formulation and testing of scientific hypotheses. I will try to describe and defend my own therapeutic posture and some of the tactical variations that flow from it in my efforts to understand and help the people who seek my assistance.

Is There a Logic of Discovery?

Discovery Versus Justification—Let me begin by drawing your attention to a certain imbalance in scientific methodology, namely, the fact that we have a great mass of machinery and techniques for testing hypotheses but only our own imaginative intelligence with which to create hypotheses to test. Thus Reichenbach (1951) in discussing his now well-known distinction between the context of discovery and the context of justification, says (p. 231):

> The act of discovery escapes logical analysis; there are no logical rules in terms of which a "discovery machine" could be constructed that would take over the creative function of the genius. . . . In other words, logic is concerned only with the context of justification.

This viewpoint is hardly a modern novelty. Abraham Kaplan (1964) cited J. S. Mill's *Logic* as follows: "Invention, though it can be cultivated, cannot be reduced to rule; there is no science which will enable a man to bethink himself of that which will suit his purpose." And F. S. C. Northrop (1947, p. 6) interprets Francis Bacon's sixteenth-century *Novum Organum* as indicating "all '*Anticipations of Nature*,' i.e., all hypotheses, are to be rejected as 'rash or premature.' Also formal logic is to be rejected since it tends to 'fix and give stability' to old errors."

Bacon was something of an Elizabethan "dust bowl" empiricist. He would have been a natural prospect for graduate study at Minnesota. He was inclined toward that philosophy of science which some of Donald Paterson's students ascribe to their mentor: if one will only collect enough data, and squeeze it hard enough, truth will emerge.

Just to nail down this idea about discovery, I would like to point out that Karl Popper also sees hypothesis formation as a nonlogical activity. Popper often presents a contrast to other logical empiricists, but in his classic study *The Logic of Scientific Discovery* (1961) we find the following (p. 31):

> The initial stage, the act of conceiving or inventing a theory, seems to me neither to call for logical analysis nor to be susceptible of it. The question how it happens that a new idea occurs to a man—whether it is a musical theme, a dramatic conflict, or a scientific theory—may be of great interest to empirical psychology; but it is irrelevant to the logical analysis of scientific knowledge.

It is a bit frightening to contemplate the vast machinery of statistical inference, mathematical analysis, symbolic logic, etc., and the world's tons of high-speed data-processing equipment, all of them dependent for input on the inspired guesswork of that peculiar assortment of people we generally lump together as "scientists."

Still, this is what our best methodological minds are telling us. Hypothesis formation is a psychological event, not a matter of inference from either propositions or experience (or from experience of propositions). This is not to say that the connections between experience and hypotheses are chaotic, but that the connections are *causal*, not logical.

Nomothetic Versus Idiographic Discovery—At this point we should note that not all hypotheses are of equal value. In fact, to be scientifically useful, a conjecture must be statable as a rather special kind of proposal. In brief, to be scientifically meaningful, a hypothesis must be stated as an empirically testable proposition. One must be able to specify data, collectible in principle, which would corroborate or impeach the proposal. There are technical arguments about confirmability versus falsifiability as the more desirable characteristic of scientific statements, but the general requirement of empirical testability is seldom, if ever, seriously questioned any longer.

The clarifications of scientific methodology springing from philosophy's preoccupation with linguistic analysis have profoundly affected the development of psychology. Behavioral scientists have always been acutely self-conscious about method, but the influence of logical positivism–empirical operationism has made us scrupulous beyond belief (particularly when combined with solid statistical training). In cold fact, our critical tools are so good that it is next to impossible to design a nontrivial experiment that does not have serious (often fatal) flaws.

Let me hasten to add that I view this situation as satisfactory in general, but unhappy in some particulars. For example, it does seem to me that our methodological sophistication encourages research which is more specialized than our real interests, since the often imprecise data and methods of study entailed in complicated psychological problems lead to a high risk of nonpublishability. But this kind of trouble—what some have called the inverse relationship between rigor and interest—is preferable to a naïveté that would delude us into believing faulty research procedures sound.

The new philosophical viewpoint in psychology probably began with our discovery of Bridgman (1928, 1936) and his discussion of the impact of logic on modern physics. It really became accepted doctrine with the publication of a classic paper by S. S. Stevens (1939) and psychology is now heavily invested in a model of science closely resembling that of the older natural sciences.

Among other things, this means that the process of scientific discovery in psychology is likely to resemble the process in physics, chemistry, etc. It is beautifully described in T. S. Kuhn's book *The Structure of Scientific Revolutions* (1962). In discussing the role of anomaly in discovery, Kuhn says (pp. 64–65):

> Further development, therefore, ordinarily calls for the construction of elaborate equipment, the development of an esoteric vocabulary and skills, and a refinement of concepts that increasingly lessens their resemblance to their usual commonsense prototypes. That professionalization leads, on the one hand, to an immense restriction of the scientist's vision and to a considerable resistance to paradigm change. The science has become increasingly rigid. On the other hand, within those areas to which the paradigm directs the attention of the group, normal science leads to a detail of information and to a precision of the observation-theory match that could be achieved in no other way. Furthermore, that detail and precision-of-match have a value that transcends their not always very high intrinsic interest. Without the special apparatus that is constructed mainly for anticipated functions, the results that lead ultimately to novelty could not occur. And even when the apparatus exists, novelty ordinarily emerges only for the man who, knowing *with precision* what he should expect, is able to recognize that something has gone wrong. Anomaly appears only against the background provided by the paradigm. The more precise and far-reaching that paradigm is, the more sensitive an indicator it provides of anomaly and hence of an occasion for paradigm change.

The sensitivity to anomaly described by Kuhn is an example of scientific artistry, a subjective sensitivity that has not been much studied. It is easily contaminated by, or confused with, ideological preconceptions, as I have tried to show elsewhere (Vance, 1962), but such sensitivity is clearly an essential part of the methodology of science.

It is at this point that a scientist-clinician is most likely to go astray, in my view. The temptation is to identify the process of formulating and testing treatment ideas with the process of formulating and testing scientific hypotheses. I do not understand the world this way.

My hunch that some of you might be irritated with me before I said a word could be treated as a scientific hypothesis. If confirmed, that conjecture might lend some support to a general theory of speech-instigated irritation (or Vance-instigated irritation). However, my interest in your state of mind is not theoretical or scientific. It is, for me, an applied and technical concern, *related to this particular and unique situation*. Furthermore, my problem does not involve the truth of the proposition that some of you are (or were) irritated so much as what I should be doing about it. In short, I am looking for a plan of action, not a fact of nature.

Another way to express this is to say that I am seeking an imperative. I want to know what I *ought* to do, but there is no way to infer imperatives from a set of declarative sentences (propositions).

Gordon Allport has dealt at length with the problem of understanding and working with individuality. In his classic study of personality (Allport, 1937) Allport borrowed the distinction between nomothetic and idiographic disciplines from the German philosopher Windelband to describe one aspect of the distinction that I am concerned with. But Allport sees Windelband's account as too radical (p. 22):

> The dichotomy, however, is too sharp: it requires a psychology divided against itself. As in the case of the two psychologies (the analytical and the descriptive) advocated by Dilthey and Spranger, the division is too drastic. It is more helpful to regard the two methods as overlapping and as contributing to one another. In the field of medicine, diagnosis and therapy are idiographic procedures, but both rest intimately upon a knowledge of the common factors in disease, determined by the nomothetic sciences of bacteriology and bio-chemistry. Likewise, biography is clearly idiographic, and yet in the best biographies one finds an artful blend of generalization with individual portraiture. A complete study of the individual will embrace both approaches.

Allport's view of psychological method proposed that both the study of general principles and studies of individual cases are essential to a scientific understanding of human behavior and experience. Unfortunately, for present purposes, both Allport's 1937 book and its sequel of a quarter-century later (Allport, 1961) are preoccupied with defending the legitimacy of unique situations as scientific subject matter, rather than explicating the logic of idiographic discovery and its relation to action. Still, Allport often indicates the general nature of the latter process. He says, for example (p. 10):

> ... the behavior of every individual is lawful in its own right. We do not have to understand every life in order to discover the lawful regularities in one life. If you have an intimate friend, you may know very well why he behaves as he does, and be able to predict and partially to control his behavior in the future, just because you know the lawful regularities in his life. You do not need a knowledge of human nature in general in order to do so.

As used in this quotation, the word "know" connotes an empathic understanding leading to correct predictions and successful strategies of influence. Idiographic knowledge, even for Allport, would appear to rest on a pragmatic basis. It is concerned with what works, what is vindicated in action, rather than what is verified by controlled observation.

"To know," in this sense is "to understand," in the way that the psychology of Verstehen uses the term. Abel (1948) has discussed this method of knowing at length. He describes Verstehen as "based on the application of personal experience to observed behavior. We 'understand' an observed or assumed connection if we are able to parallel either one with something we know though self-observation does happen" (p. 216).

The value of such a method is not in its production of new knowledge, since, as Abel points out, this procedure is not a method of verification. Abel concludes that logical limitations

> ... virtually preclude the use of the operation of Verstehen as a scientific tool of analysis. Still there is one positive function which the operation can perform in scientific investigations: It can serve as an aid in preliminary explorations of a subject. Furthermore the operation can be particularly helpful in setting up hypotheses, even though it cannot be used to test them.

Abel is another theoretician who sees the difficulty in dealing with the process of hypothesis formulation but is satisfied to leave it unexplored because it is not a part of the methodological analysis of factual verification. Methodologists are apparently content that there is no shortage of hypothesis in the intellectual marketplace.

Some Characteristics of the Market for Theories

Insofar as theories are tools to be used rather than pedagogical devices to be discarded at the end of one's training, intellectual status symbols, or recreational materials (games to be played), consumer response will be related to factors such as effectiveness, convenience, compatibility with other tools, cost, etc.

This economic analogy is not entirely a rhetorical device. The marketplace concept of the world of ideas has been seriously explored by a number of investigators. For example, Machlup (1962) has attempted a general economic analysis of the market for knowledge of all sorts in the United States. I have adopted the marketing analogy because I wish to draw attention to the variety of possible determinants of theory choice, particularly those not directly related to validity, in order to examine the influence of users on the development of theories of therapy.

Clinical practitioners make up a reasonably identifiable group of theory consumers. Studies by the Mental Health Manpower Studies Unit (1964, 1965) within the National Institute of Mental Health provide some data about this group, at least those members working in hospitals, clinics, and other mental health establishments. There are about 8,000 psychiatrists, 3,000 residents, 4,000 other physicians, 6,000 psychologists, and 8,000 social workers. Also, while these 29,000 people are consuming theories, over 100,000 aides and 20,000 nurses are caring for the patients. Private practice probably accounts for another 6,000 psychiatrists, 2,000 psychologists, and some social workers too. Altogether, excluding the nurses and aides, something like 40,000 consumers are in this cluster. I do not believe that equivalent data exist for the manpower situation in counseling, guidance, and student personnel work, but what I do know suggests that another 40,000 or more theory consumers exist in these fields.

The import of all this is that there are very few highly professional practitioners in the theory market. An estimate of 100,000 would be exceedingly generous for this group, whereas there are several million people who have a minor or peripheral interest in theories of counseling and psychotherapy. Teachers, general medical practitioners, undergraduate students in the behavioral sciences, interested research scientists, administrators, and curious laymen make up a much larger group than the people in some form of counseling or psychotherapy practice.

Such a situation generates a heavy demand for survey and introductory materials as opposed to interest in advanced and specialized works. In consequence, books concerning theories of therapy are usually directed away from practitioner needs altogether, or else they are pitched at the most general level of interest.

Book-length studies in depth of specialized approaches are rare. However, they do exist, as, for example, Fenichel (1945), Fromm-Reichmann (1950), Rogers' series of volumes (1942, 1951, 1961), and Wolpe (1958). Journals would seem to be a natural outlet for the exchange of technical information about counseling and psychotherapy, but case materials are wordy and there is no standardized mode of presentation for clinical data. When one also considers editorial needs for rigor and brevity, it is not surprising that the periodical literature is a nightmare combination of the incomprehensible and inconsequential, with an occasional gem to repay a patient reader.

In any case, publication lags make both books and journals suitable for archival use only. Published materials, as we now have them in this field, are no help in increasing one's therapeutic skills, and they are of limited value in the initial stages of training. I have no hard evidence that reading has actually harmed beginning counselors or therapists, but I believe it is so. I have certainly had the experience of being forced to uneducate trainees so they could begin to learn from their practicum experience.

To sum up this matter of the marketplace for clinical ideas, let me say bluntly that the size and mixture of the market does not produce materials that are really good for people who want to acquire and develop clinical skills. Those of us really concerned about training practitioners are living in a world where our skills are transmitted by an oral tradition supplemented by crude techniques of mutual observation and criticism. The remainder of my presentation is concerned with examining some aspects of this oral tradition, because I see no hope that we can support a more sophisticated process in the near future.

Distribution Points for Techniques of Therapy

The practitioner ordinarily acquires his theoretical equipment in bits and pieces. It is like becoming a hi-fi bug, or a ham operator, or a car customizer, or like building a house and constantly changing the blueprints as you go along. From the first moment of the first time that you sit down with a person labeled "patient" or "client" you become engaged in a building, tinkering, testing, scrapping, revising, sweating, and cursing experience.

The beginner in this business is almost certain to acquire his first theoretical kit as a kind of gift. Exposure to a survey of all kinds of theories may be involved, but the first practicum supervisor is in a powerful position of influence and provides the first working model to the budding clinician. If this first mentor is what I think of as good, the neophyte will learn fast not to get preoccupied with the sophistication and elegance of his theoretical machinery but will be confronted again and again with the question Does it work? and If not, why not?

It is my view that the need for clinically workable ideas markedly changes the quality of one's attention to discussions of theory. The data a therapist needs to organize are likely to be those with which the theory developer also deals; however, the therapist needs to organize this information for action, not for factual understanding. My kind of therapist is constantly worried about three things: (1) What is going on? (2) What should be going on? (3) What can I do to help it happen? It is very important to observe that only the first of these questions can be answered by a set of declarative sentences. Questions 2 and 3 call for some imperatives, and, I repeat, there is no form of logical inference that leads from descriptive, declarative premises to imperative conclusions. One must have some theoretically prescribed goals and procedural rules to function in this way (although clients or patients often prescribe goals and may even suggest techniques).

In addition to theoretical machinery, one needs practice in using it, preferably with consultation available from experienced hands. This gets us back again to the oral-tradition aspect of therapy training and also suggests why clinicians are so gregarious. Much of the advanced training of psychotherapists consists in sharing experiences with colleagues. I am convinced that the regionalism that exists in theory and practice is determined by the fact that the only really effective channel now available for distributing clinically useful information is word-of-mouth.

Clinical Training as a Kind of Consumer Education

If pressed for a label, I call myself an empirical clinician. The materials outlining the positions to be discussed in this conference propose the label "pragmatic-empirical" for my style of practice. The fact that I do rather like both of these labels suggests that they are suitable. But what do they mean?

Perhaps I can begin to clarify my posture by making some remarks about training.

It is my belief that practicum experience should involve students in a variety of approaches to treatment problems. I find it inconceivable that all client concerns can best be formulated within a single theoretical model, or that every kind of distress will be treated optimally by any single clinical method.

This implies that training cannot be done adequately in any setting that does not have enough variety of clientele and flexibility of staff to provide meaningful experience across types of clients and types of treatment. I *really* mean that I don't consider anything less to be real professional training qualifying a person to engage in the unsupervised practice of counseling or psychotherapy.

It is interesting to me that Rogers in a recent statement (1966) has indicated a need for some modification of premises and treatment procedures related to the diagnostic status of patients. His ideas have occupied a unique and complicated place among approaches to treatment, in large measure because of his insistence that the processes of change and the techniques for facilitating change are identical for all situations.

The client-centered point of view has a number of distinguishing characteristics. These include the developing hypothesis that certain attitudes in the therapist constitute the necessary and sufficient conditions of therapeutic effectiveness. [Rogers, 1966, p. 188.]

. . . the hypothesis that the same principles of psychotherapy apply to the competently functioning business executive, the maladjusted and the neurotic person who comes to a clinic, and the hospitalized psychotic on the back ward. [Rogers, 1966, p. 184.]

The hairline crack in this position appears thus:

Very tentatively it appears to me at the present time that, in dealing with the extremely immature or regressed individual, a conditional regard may be more effective in getting a relationship under way, hence therapy under way, than unconditional positive regard. It seems clear that some immature or regressed clients may perceive a conditional caring as constituting more acceptance than an unconditional caring. The therapist who expresses the theme, "I don't like it when you act in such and such a way: I care for you more when you act in a more grownup fashion" may be perceived as a "better parent" than one whose caring is unconditional. [Rogers, 1966, p. 186.]

I quote Rogers at length because I see him as the only serious critic of the idea that people have a variety of ways of going wrong with themselves and require a variety of processes to get better.

The beginning clinician needs to know what is available in the published marketplace of ideas and in the oral traditions of his craft. He would be well advised to train and take his first professional position in a large and complex setting. In two or three years of steady practice, he can acquire enough experience with client and theory variables to make informed commitments that will shape the growth of his skills during the rest of his career.

What Does a Pragmatic-Empirical Approach Look Like?

I believe it is expected that I directly expose more of my own orientation than can be seen in the earlier parts of this discussion.

Let me outline my experience as a practitioner. I apprenticed as a clinical psychology trainee with the Veterans Administration. This means that, as a graduate student, I worked approximately 1,000 hours in the psychiatric section of a general hospital and about 2,000 hours in an outpatient clinic and about 1,000 hours as an intern in a neuropsychiatric hospital. I also spent nine months, quarter time, in the child psychiatry section of a university hospital.

My full-time professional employment has included six years in a college counseling center and two years away from any practice in an administrative job, and I am currently in my second year as a combination clinician-administrator. During the time indicated, I have had more than 6,000 interviews with about 3,000 people in connection with concerns covering the whole range of clinical syndromes, plus vocational guidance, educational planning, family pathology, and a bit of child guidance.

My reason for engaging in this flagrant bit of horn tooting is to establish that I am speaking as a practitioner. I have done, and am still doing, the things we are talking about, and, if we are going to get into arguments of the "I knew a client once" variety, I want it understood that I've seen my share, and maybe more. Also, I know that it is not generally the case that qualified people continue to practice counseling and psychotherapy. It is fatiguing, often dull, not prestigious, academically self-defeating, and occasionally rewarding beyond measure.

But how does a pragmatic empiricist work? I shall try to answer that question by means of an illustration.

I see a lot of students who are engaging in motivated academic failure. I don't mean underachievers. I mean bright people who see themselves behaving in ways guaranteed to result in total academic disaster but unable to do things that they know they should and that lie well within their capabilities. A common way of expressing this is to say, "I don't have any motivation," or, more insightfully, "I seem to have a will to fail."

How can I deal with such a situation? Well, with some frequency, I use one or another of four models: (1) insight psychotherapy; (2) reflective, Rogerian counseling; (3) rational-emotive therapy; or (4) a learning-theory approach to conflict resolution (avoidance reduction). I am not entirely able to articulate what the cues are that suggest to me that one rather than another of these formulations is more appropriate. I know that available time, manifest anxiety, verbal fluency of the client, family dynamics, and specificity of symptoms all affect the decision.

However, just for the sake of discussion, let's assume that I have a client with whom I have chosen to work on an insight-psychotherapy basis. In such a case my strategy would be to move as fast as possible toward working with the questions Why might a person wish, perhaps unconsciously wish, to fail? Is it self-punishment? An attempt to hurt others? Fear of the consequences of success? Something else? The goal is to determine what is being communicated indirectly by the symptom, deal with it directly, and thus obviate the need for the symptom. Perhaps that's oversimplified but many (not all) of the clients I treat this way get well. So do the others, and I can't detect any radical differences in my success rate across techniques.

Maybe the interviews are incidental (a ghastly placebo), and any kind of attention would do. That seems unlikely and doesn't lose me any sleep. The really troublesome thought for me is that there is some effective thing I do, regardless of what I think I'm doing, that is entirely unrelated to my stated strategy. It may even be that the residual aspects of one or another of my *rejected* strategies is the effective agent. That is, in the insight-therapy example, it may be that the client gets better because of the incidental clarification of feelings that takes place, or because of relaxation and extinction of avoidance-producing anxiety, or because the client stops believing unrealistic things about his situation without ever verbalizing them to me at all.

I find this very troublesome. The idea that I might do my best job of being like Rogers when I am working like mad to be Freud is almost too much to bear. But it does help keep one from being arrogant and, in my case, leads to more concern with getting results than with sticking to any prescribed pattern of procedure.

I hope that this sketch of my approach will help to explain my obsessive concern with the distinction between truth and effectiveness. It is my view that theories of therapy may be vindicated by clinical results even in some instances where verification of alleged factual content is impossible.

In closing, I would like to return to my hunch that at least some of you were irritated before I opened my mouth. You should now understand that I don't really wish to corroborate that notion. You may also have some insight into the fact that my expectation of resistance had a considerable impact on the amount, and I hope the quality, of work I put into this presentation. If you understand this, and if I have managed to get your attention, the hypothesis is vindicated in my book, whether it was valid or not.

After all, it *is* results that interest a pragmatic-empiricist, and I really am beginning to like the label.

References

Abel, T.   The operation called *verstehen*. *American Journal of Sociology*, 1948, 54, 211–218.

Allport, Gordon W.   *Personality.* New York: Holt, 1937.

Allport, Gordon W.   *Pattern and Growth in Personality.* New York: Holt, Rinehart & Winston, 1961.

Bridgman, P. W.   *The Nature of Physical Theory.* Princeton, N.J.: Princeton University Press, 1936.

Bridgman, P. W.   *The Logic of Modern Physics.* New York: Macmillan, 1928.

Fenichel, O.   *The Psychoanalytic Theory of Neurosis.* New York: Norton, 1945.

Fromm-Reichmann, F.   *Principles of Intensive Psychotherapy.* Chicago: University of Chicago Press, 1950.

Kaplan, Abraham.   *The Conduct of Inquiry.* San Francisco: Chandler, 1964.

Kuhn, Thomas S.   *The Structure of Scientific Revolutions.* Chicago: University of Chicago Press, 1962.

Machlup, Fritz.   *The Production and Distribution of Knowledge.* Princeton, N.J.: Princeton University Press, 1962.

Mental Health Manpower Studies Unit, Current Statistical and Activities Report. No. 1, Jan.–Mar., 1964: Estimated total number of professional personnel employed in mental health establishments for selected professional classifications, 1963.

Mental Health Manpower Studies Unit, Current Statistical and Activities Report. No. 3, Oct., 1964: Selected characteristics of psychiatrists in the U.S.

Mental Health Manpower Studies Unit, Current Statistical and Activities Report. No. 4, Feb., 1965: Selected characteristics of psychologists employed in mental health establishments, 1963.

Northrop, F. S. C. *The Logic of the Sciences and the Humanities.* New York: Macmillan, 1947.

Popper, K. R. *The Logic of Scientific Discovery.* New York: Basic Books, 1961.

Reichenbach, Hans. *The Rise of Scientific Philosophy.* Berkeley: University of California Press, 1951.

Rogers, Carl R. *Counseling and Psychotherapy.* Boston: Houghton Mifflin, 1942.

Rogers, Carl R. *Client-Centered Therapy.* Boston: Houghton Mifflin, 1951.

Rogers, Carl R. *On Becoming a Person: A Therapist's View of Psychotherapy.* Boston: Houghton Mifflin, 1961.

Rogers, Carl R. Client-centered therapy. In S. Arieti (ed.), *American Handbook of Psychiatry,* Vol. III. Chap. 13. New York: Basic Books, 1966.

Stevens, S. S. Psychology and the science of science. *Psychological Bulletin,* 1939, 36, 221–263.

Vance, F. L. Methodology versus ideology in psychological research. *Journal of Counseling Psychology,* 1962, 9, 12–17.

Wolpe, J. *Psychotherapy by Reciprocal Inhibition.* Stanford, Cal.: Stanford University Press, 1958.

Shall We Compartmentalize
Thought and Action?

EDWARD S. BORDIN
University of Michigan

Evidently the planners of this conference chose the discussants of the invited papers with a view to controversy. The label attached to the paper assigned to me is "pragmatic empiricism." This makes me wonder whether I am to represent impractical theorists! Seriously, I absolve the planners of any *ad hominem* intent, but I do sense at some points in Vance's paper a tendency to separate theory from practice. He seems to be saying, "A clinician has practical things to do to or with persons, and theory has nothing to contribute to that enterprise." Since at other points he appears to accept the usefulness of theory —e.g., he insists that the student clinician have many supervisors representing different theories and approaches to treatment, and describes himself as eclectic in relying on four different theories—I will not give much time to the position that the most sophisticated form of practice is that nourished by the interaction of theory and observation. Being pragmatic too often stands for taking action not because we know what to do but because an action is demanded willy-nilly. Too often the hurried search for something that "works" and its vindication is illusory in that the only goals attained by either party are those of permitting a mutually acceptable extrication from a relationship.

Understanding and action are not antithetical. Let me use a concrete example. I *was* irritated as I began to read Vance's paper. Vance might have said, "The way to irritate Ed Bordin is to use such phrases as 'psychological interview' and 'discovery machine.'" Now if any useful purpose can be served by either irritating me or avoiding the same, it is important to understand that I was irritated because Vance had procrastinated so long in preparing his paper that I was left too little time to prepare my comment. Understanding, if it lives up to its name, connotes that intimate knowledge of events which permits us to influence their course. Theories are understanding broadened to encompass classes of individuals and categories of events. Good theories are those that translate into action.

The Place of Theory

I turn now to a more general examination of Vance's argument. In essence he marshals a series of propositions designed to lead us to the conclusion that concern with theory is best kept in the background of the education of the counselor or psychotherapist. He approaches the position that the only significant influence of a theory rests in its expression by the supervisor acting as a model. His argument actually divides into two somewhat contradictory sections. In the first section he asserts that concern with an individual separates counseling from science because (1) we are seeking to discover something about the individual, and discovery is not logical; (2) we are seeking plans of action rather than the facts of nature; (3) we need to know the lawful regularities of a specific individual rather than of human nature. In the second section, implicitly accepting that theories are applicable, he argues that reading and, presumably, thinking about theories is harmful. The only way to learn is by practice and oral communication with other, preferably more experienced, clinicians.

Taking up each of his assertions in turn, I suggest that discovery of the generalization regarding an individual is not quite the same as discovery in science, though under certain conditions they may coincide. If we have reasonably precise knowledge regarding a behavioral phenomenon, our study of the individual involves an examination of which of the known factors in the phenomenon are present in his case. This knowledge coupled with our general knowledge then guides our actions. When our general knowledge is fragmentary and imprecise, as is so often the case, then we truly approach the process of discovery of which Vance speaks, but we had better be equally sensitive to the process of verification so that we don't go off half-cocked in response to every transitory intuition.

His separation of plans of action from the facts of nature has already been commented on. I can only add that I hope that the next time he plans to fly he does not overlook the fact of nature that man's arms cannot function like a bird's wings!

Similarly, my reactions to the separation of generalizations about individuals and about people have already been registered. The generalizations about an individual must be consistent with the generalizations about persons. When such generalizations conflict, one or the other must be re-examined. The fact of generalizations about human nature no more obviates the need for a clinical study of the individual than knowledge of physical laws does away with the careful study of terrain, climate, etc., that an engineer or architect must engage in as part of the process of erecting a bridge or a building.

My position, then, is that intimate knowledge of theories must be integrated with the developed art of action in the most effectively functioning counselor or psychotherapist. Vance is worried about two pitfalls. One is that the counselor treats the mastery of his craft as a purely intellectual process, neglecting to translate his theory into action or maintaining a compartmentalization of theory and action. The other is that the counselor becomes the prisoner of his theoretical commitment. I agree that these concerns are not to be taken lightly, but I do not accept the remedy, which is, I fear, to provide the student with a superficial smattering of theories so that he escapes infection.

The Use of Theory

My remedy starts with the assumption that concepts are best understood when they are founded in direct commerce with the phenomena toward which the concepts are directed. The time for the student to give serious study to theories of personality and psychopathology and to theories of treatment is as he is accumulating observations of persons. He examines theories of personality while he is receiving field experience in trying to assess persons. His study of theories of counseling and psychotherapy accompanies work in counseling relationships. Unlike Vance, I want the student to become directly acquainted with the theory in its original form rather than by word of mouth. It is important to learn how others interpret and act according to the theory, but the serious study of the formal theory should not be neglected.

To avoid a defensive attachment to a particular theory, we must understand what makes the student defensive. Therapeutic work represents a "building, tinkering, testing . . . sweating, and cursing experience," to use Vance's vivid language. There is no escaping this existential anxiety, which stimulates some to reduce it by seeking pseudo certainty in close adherence to a single view of man. We should not overlook the fact that distancing oneself in the nihilistic postures that nothing is known is another avenue of escape. We teachers must urge and encourage the student to tolerate the anxiety rather than seek an escape. Instead of presenting a survey of theories as museum pieces, we must engage him in the ongoing search for deeper, more precise understanding for which current theories are the available approximations. As clinical supervisors we must teach him to use theories to nourish his observations and to use his observations to modify or extend his theories. We must disclose to him those times when he seeks to give up the struggle by saying that all theories are tenable without recognizing where they are compatible and where contradictory.

While I am sympathetic with Vance's requirement that the student have experience with a variety of approaches to treatment problems, I am equally concerned that he have a thoroughgoing experience with at least one. To me this means that it is undesirable for the student to shuttle from one supervisor to another. If there is time, let him have successive immersion in more than one model of treatment, but always accompanied by acquaintance with other models supplied by the presence of clinicians of other stripes in the field agency, supplemented by readings and by motion-picture-recorded or electrical-tape-recorded interviews conducted from other orientations.

It is clear that we share as the ultimate goal the development of a clinician who above all can respond to another person with insight and empathy and in a way that meets his need for change. I suspect that Vance and I are similarly wary of too great an emphasis on the verification of abstract implications of theories. The sharpest area of disagreement seems to lie in my believing that the knowledge base that scientist and clinician seek is the same. Sharp differences make interesting conferences.

The Encounter

One of the concepts we had in planning the seminar was that the counselor must be able to generate evidence from his own experience regarding his effectiveness. His continued growth seemed to us to depend upon that. With this concept in mind I initiated the discussion with my question to Dr. Vance, and it led us back to some of the considerations regarding the deduction of imperatives that he discussed in his paper. From there it was rather natural to raise several questions about the preparations of counselors, terminating in a reaffirmation of Dr. Vance's position that the way to learn to do counseling is by doing it under the supervision of a variety of persons.

PARKER: How do you decide that your clinical judgment was a good one? How do you know that what you do is effective?

VANCE: The proof of the pudding is not in the immediate eating. It is how the digestive process feels later on. What you are really talking about is how to develop some confidence in what you are doing. That takes a while; you have to have some long-term follow-up. This spring I got a letter from someone I saw almost ten years ago saying, "I'm still doing fine." He didn't say it was my fault, but I ascribe some of the result to me. This was a client whom I saw over a period of six years. Through great tenacity we managed to keep him alive, literally. He was a person who had made suicidal gestures and who now, ten years later, is still alive. He is now reporting that it is a good thing to be alive. Part of this result was due to being attentive. When that kind of patient misses an appointment, you find out where he is and if he is not available you alert his parents. I have no hesitancy about doing so in such a situation. We found this particular person in a distant city contemplating an act. We had him brought back. You cannot get feedback on his kind of person overnight, and you don't get feedback in every case.

PARKER: You mentioned in your paper that such long-term successes may just be due to the placebo. How do you know?

127

VANCE: The people I'm most likely to be in conflict with are those who believe that therapy and medicine are really scientific rather than artistic endeavors—people who think that factual content leads rather directly to successful intervention. I was very clearly nurtured on the idea that if you understood a theory of personality in some detail you would be able, as you worked with people, to fit them into the conceptual apparatus and that this would give you rather direct indications for action.

It has only dawned on me in the past two or three years that there is a fallacy in this. When you want a rule for action that is imperative in form, even "Open the window," the question of how to arrive at such an imperative is a very touchy matter. There is just no way to go logically from a set of facts, propositions about nature, or declarative sentences to an imperative kind of statement. Technique, then, is very different from science. When you are confronted with anything that calls for action, you have to deal with more than facts. You don't act on the basis of syllogisms. There is no way to articulate verbally what happens because the transition from thinking to action is not verbal.

BACH: Except that you can describe how, as a therapist, you *get there*. I think I can best describe me as a therapist by use of an actual situation with a patient, or with a family. You seem to deny the fact that there are ways of proceeding that have some things in common that you can share from therapist to patient. You can also share from supervisor to supervisee, who can then use those things in a new set of therapeutic situations. This is how training occurs.

VANCE: I think it is a matter of imitation. It came up in three of the other papers. People mentioned that one of the best ways to learn is to do co-therapy—to actually be in the room. I get trainees at a point where they have had a certain amount of didactic instruction, but they have no sense of how or whether any of these things will work in dealing with people. One of the most convincing experiences they can have is to sit in the room while therapy is going on or view it through a window. Therapy has something akin to taking out an appendix, or swimming, or riding a bicycle. You can read about it, you can get all the theory down, but you cannot then automatically do it. I really mean it when I say that if we had better technical observation facilities I think we could more completely communicate because what we are teaching is *technique*.

Dr. Vance and Dr. Bach exchanged some of their own ideas about what goes on "inside" the therapist during an interview. It was clear that both conceptualized the client's situation in terms that are communicable either by some standard theoretical system or in more idiographic terms. Dr. Bach explained that he has often found it helpful to communicate his own cognitions through questions, explanations, or formulations to clients or teachers. Dr. Vance, on the other hand, expressed a general reluctance to do this with trainees because of their tendency to accept prematurely "his system" as "the system." As trainees gained more experience, he felt, it was more possible. In fact, he pointed to his own experience as one of wide exposure to many points of view in just this way.

VANCE: There was one point Bordin made in his paper that I feel compelled to comment on: his preference for preparation in depth in at least one theoretical model. This is very hard to quarrel with except on practical grounds. In training, at least as I have experienced it and as I suspect it is still going on, the instruction and supervision in actual interview activity is dispersed across people. I reflected on my own set of supervisors, and it is a horrendous long list. My recollection of that experience is a kind of horrible impinging of multiple conceptual frameworks with no central core I would care to identify. This was not accidental. The particular set of classmates I had approached the faculty and asked, "Why is it that there is no course offered in therapy?" After discussion of an hour or so Paul Meehl finally said, "Well, to be perfectly honest, none of us would agree to let any one of the others teach such a course." So it was done with malice aforethought. I really wonder whether a place exists any longer, outside of an analytic training institute, that has a faculty with enough of a central viewpoint for a person in training to be exposed in depth to any single viewpoint.

MEMBER OF AUDIENCE: One of the things that bothers me about this model is that in my experience you get a person very, very unsure of himself. Secondly, in a one- or two-year school counselor education program I'm uncertain as to whether I can teach all of these things. Would you comment about that?

VANCE: I certainly don't think you can train anybody in two years to be a general psychological practitioner. I don't understand the function of the school counselor terribly well. These people have got to be limited practitioners of some sort, don't they? I don't think anybody would feel comfortable saying that the product of even the best two-year counselor education program should engage in unsupervised general practice of psychotherapy.

PATTERSON: I'll take that position. I think my people after three semesters of training are better prepared in psychotherapy than some clinical psychologists coming out of any school in the country.

VANCE: I don't know about any school. But there are some schools that have an anti-therapy training program. On the other hand, I can think of three or four schools on the east coast which probably produce better-qualified people than you could get in a one-year or two-year program. There are some awfully confusing kinds of conditions where you do need a modicum of diagnostic skill, and where there is a real potential for personal disaster. I can't really believe people trained in two years are adequately prepared to identify subtly schizophrenic people who are capable of real spasms of totally disorganized behavior. Nor can I believe such persons are tooled into the professional community in such a way as to accept total responsibility for case management.

BACH: I disagree very strongly with that position. I think you can train school counselors in a short time to use themselves clearly enough to know when they are in the presence of someone who is schizophrenic. I was with a group of senior high school counselors for the first time and they were talking about more disturbed cases than I see in my office constantly. One asked, "What do I do with a kid that says to me, 'My hands aren't my own. I feel as if I'm not in my body.'?" I said, "Did you try holding his hand?" He said, "No, I can't do that. I'm a school counselor and I don't have a right to touch kids!" We went through some issues on that! I said, "Why not?" "Well,

I'm too scared" is what really came out. "I have to refer to somebody who is expert." I said, "What kind of experts do you know who deal with schizophrenia?" There isn't anybody that I know, and I do as much work with schizophrenic families over a long period of time as anybody does. There are no nice psychotherapeutic answers for this kind of problem even though we know a lot about such families and their actions.

Inherent in your position is a limiting factor that exists in training programs all over the country. That limiting factor is, You can only go so far and no farther. We scheduled family interviews for a counselor who had three students in various grades in high school with whom he was having problems. He set up regular family interviews with the father, mother, and five children for several purposes. One of the purposes was to reach an educational contract for how they can teach their kids and the kids can stay in school. That may be a pretty minimal thing, but this family sounds like as nutty a family as I would ever see. The rules in that family that are designed to make these kids poor functioners are tremendous. If the counselor starts on a very simplistic basis, recognizing that some things are going to happen that will be over his head, then he has some learning to do for himself but he can be helpful meanwhile. He also has to find out whom he can see when he gets into a panic. Of course, you have to build in more supervisory time, but they can learn. Your answer to the question tends to limit and make hopeless this kind of situation even if that is not your intent.

VANCE: Dr. Patterson said his people *are* trained this way. You said they *can* be trained this way. I want to know if they *should* be trained this way, given the things that need to go on within the focus of the school.

MEMBER OF AUDIENCE: My question has to do with the proper mix between the didactic and the practical. I got the impression from your paper that too much knowledge is a dangerous thing; too much knowledge is bad. This certainly is not very consistent with most of the other things in higher education.

VANCE: Yes, I really believe, and I tried to be as frank as I could in that, that my experience with clinical students who have had between a year and two years of work before they see a patient for whom they have any kind of clinical responsibility has been an unhappy one. They come to their first contact with patients in so spastic a condition that they are almost immobilized. Those that I have seen who begin to have some kind of meaningful interaction with patients some place in the first semester are much less traumatized and have much less emotional blockage. They also do a much better job of digesting the theoretical training.

5

Counselor Education:
Facilitating the Development
of a Helping Person

DONALD H. BLOCHER
University of Minnesota

The past fifteen years have witnessed the evolution of a series of dramatic changes in the conceptualization of counseling, and of psychotherapy. Formerly cherished notions of the counselor as a passive, shadowy acceptor and reflector of feelings and opinions have gradually given way to an image of the counselor as an active and dynamic agent of change in the lives of those with whom he engages in therapeutic encounter.

Concepts of congruence and confrontation, transparency and authenticity have replaced the older images of neutrality and objectivity as the *sine qua non* of helping relationships. Perhaps even that beloved and unfailingly innocuous "uh-huh" is no longer considered the modal response of the well-bred counselor. Instead, counselors have begun to admit and even to prize their abilities to influence values and to change behavior. The twenty-year orgy of handwringing by counselors over the presumed ethical dilemmas involved in the "directive" versus "non-directive" pseudo issue has finally about run to extinction.

The transformation which is the culmination of those changes might well be called the defeminization of counseling. To rebut Farson's old phrase, the counselor is no longer a woman. This change in the Zeitgeist is readily apparent in the recent literature. Stieper and Wiener (1965), for example, talk unflinchingly of the "power factors" in therapy and of creating "bind" situations from which clients are forced to learn new ways of coping with interpersonal situations. Krumboltz, perhaps a bit ostentatiously, terms the impact of behavioral approaches the "Revolution in Counseling." Kell and Mueller (1967) summarize the new order of things when they say that "the process of counseling is a continual testing of the counselor's adequacy" (p. 15). They go on to point out that freedom from ambivalence, insecurity, and guilt about the relationship is essential for effective counselor behavior.

Unfortunately, if not unpredictably, this shift in conceptualization has left counselor education largely unprepared to meet the challenge. The essence of the change has been to offer counselor education the opportunity to put the emphasis back where it belongs, on education. If education at its best is liberating in intent and integrating in effect, then the challenge of preparing counselors today is truly an educational one.

The past two decades have seen an emphasis on "training" counselors rather than educating them. Counselors have been variously given a set of fixed techniques which they were instructed to apply in rigid ways, or taught to think solely within the confines of narrowly conceived theoretical approaches, or expected to dispense test results and other information in mechanical fashions justified by their so-called objectivity.

These kinds of counseling and counselor education approaches have sustained themselves on the most meager of intellectual diets. Although supposedly a psychologically based professional activity, counseling has not drawn much sustenance from psychological disciplines. Counselor educators themselves have hardly been a group distinguished by psychological sophistication or affiliation. A recent survey by the Association for Counselor Education and Supervision (1967), for example, indicates that only half the counselor educators are affiliated with APA and only one-fourth hold their highest degree in some branch of psychology.

If any intellectual thread holds the counselor education enterprise together it is a philosophical rather than a psychological one. In many respects even the philosophical underpinnings of counselor education have been largely a rather sophomoric adherence to a creed of love and kindness which has been hard to dignify as especially unique or perspicacious, even with yeoman efforts to bring it under the mystical mantle of that most fashionable of philosophies, existentialism.

One reason for the failure of counselor education to build a firm foundation on the discipline of psychology has been its inability to look in the right places for support. For the past twenty or more years counselor education has pursued a very distant but hardly platonic infatuation with psychiatry. Personality theory, that romantic if ephemeral will-o'-the-wisp, which has succeeded only in translating the speculations of philosophy into the jargon of psychology, has been viewed as the fountainhead of psychological wisdom.

Until quite recently counselor education has steadfastly ignored the only areas of psychological endeavor to make substantial progress in the past twenty years. I mean social psychology and the psychology of learning. These two branches of psychology, particularly as they merge into experimental social psychology, have finally begun to furnish some solid evidence about the most fundamental problems of concern to counseling and counselor education. We at last are beginning to be able to understand some of the dynamics involved in how people learn from each other as social beings engaged in interpersonal relationships—which, as it turns out, are neither mystical nor mysterious.

As this new evidence starts to penetrate the parochial insulation which counselor education has imposed upon itself, new approaches and methodologies are emerging. Largely as a result of new knowledge about group dynamics we have seen group counseling change from an expedient dictated by cost consciousness to a powerful and sophisticated tool designed to utilize the tremendously strong motivational factors inherent in group cohesiveness and public commitment.

A new technology for changing human behavior has issued from the explication of simple principles of learning, and counseling has finally begun to address itself to the task of harnessing and humanizing it. Studies of human perceptual and cognitive development and of the processes by which people organize and assign meanings to events have led to much more sophisticated approaches to the design of learning experiences.

Interpersonal Relationships

Not the least important of the new learnings is in the explication of the nature of those interpersonal relationships which facilitate personal and social learning. As social psychology continues to amass evidence that human behavior is very much a product of social interaction, the specific characteristics of the types of interaction which contribute to the development of effective human behavior become paramount. Again, social psychology presents ample evidence that at least two factors in social interaction are vital determinants of the behavior of participants: involvement and communication.

When people are actively and dynamically involved in an interpersonal situation, their behavior tends to change in response to that situation. This principle has become virtually a truism in social psychology. In counseling, conditions leading to involvement have been variously termed warmth, acceptance, caring, concern, or positive regard. The considerable evidence (Truax and Carkhuff, 1967) supporting the importance of this element in interpersonal relationships which lead to learning should hardly be surprising.

Similarly, behavior change in individuals operating in social systems has been shown to occur as a function of the communication patterns within the system. One basic characteristic of the behavior of higher organisms is that it is maintained or modified in accordance with feedback from the environment. In interpersonal situations that feedback is the product of communication processes.

Several aspects of communication are of particular importance in counseling. One of them can be called perceptual sensitivity and applies to the counselor as a receiver of communication. Unless the receiver of communication has the sensitivity to pick up the signals emitted by others in the network, communication is limited, distorted, or lost entirely. Listening, or sensitivity, is central to counseling. A second aspect of receiving communication, however, also important, relates to the way communications are processed cognitively so that their meaning is understood. Unless counselors have cognitive structures which are open, tentative, and flexible, they may be unable to process information from clients in ways that allow real communication to occur. Taken together, perceptual sensitivity and cognitive flexibility help define the quality of empathy which has long been recognized as a major element in helping relationships.

Another aspect of communication concerns the counselor as a transmitter of communications. When people are able to convey clear unambiguous communications to others, they can serve as sources of feedback which can modify behavior. Such feedback may be termed a reinforcer since it has the power to increase the probability of occurrence of responses to which it is linked by logic or contiguity. When signals are emitted that are ambiguous, conflicting, or confusing, the resulting feedback may be inadequate to modify behavior in any consistent or purposeful way.

The ability to emit consistent, unambiguous communications is closely related to what is now called in counseling congruence, authenticity, openness, or sometimes confrontiveness. Again theory and research support the relevance of this factor to learning in interpersonal relationships.

To summarize briefly, considerable support from social psychology, psychology of learning, and recent counseling theory and research exists for the position that interpersonal involvement, perceptual sensitivity, cognitive flexibility, and consistency of communication are important factors in interpersonal learning.

The above rationale has rather profound implications for counselor educators who are responsible for designing learning experiences which will shape desirable interpersonal behaviors for counselors. Counselors in preparation are essentially people who are attempting so to improve the quality of their interpersonal relationships that they will be able to facilitate the learning of others. In learning to become a counselor an individual typically is introduced into a hierarchy of increasingly difficult interpersonal tasks which range from establishing a relaxed and secure atmosphere, to assisting toward greater self-exploration, possibly to intervening in a self-defeating pattern of social behavior. In coping with these essentially developmental tasks he acquires new patterns of interpersonal behaviors, which are what counselor education programs are intended to produce.

As counselors in preparation approach new interpersonal situations, they are in a state of dissonance, which provides the motivation for new learning. The dissonance is reduced or heightened by the feedback or reinforcement the student receives in the social system represented by the counselor education program. The sources of feedback include the counselor education staff, other students, and clients.

In coping with new interpersonal tasks, the counselor in preparation draws upon any of several resources which could in a sense be termed response modes. The crucial purpose of the counselor education program is to shape behavior within these response modes in order to produce a counselor whose integrated pattern of interpersonal behavior will allow him to function as a helping person. It is the position of this paper that each response mode is best shaped through a particular kind of learning process.

Response Mode A ; The Immediate-Intuitive

As they approach new interpersonal tasks or re-encounter old ones with new sets of expectations, counselors in preparation usually draw upon well-established patterns of social interactions which have been learned or overlearned to the point that they are at a rather low level of conscious awareness. The basis for behaving is an immediate and intuitive one; that is, it is what dimly *feels* right. If previous experience has taught the student to cope with particular kinds of situations and people according to specific patterns of behavior, these patterns will feel right and be the basis for similar behavior.

In the counselor education program several dissonance-producing situations occur to upset the equilibrium provided by a purely intuitive response mode. First efforts are directed toward making the student aware of his interpersonal behaviors and sensitizing him to feedback from others about the quality of his interpersonal relationships. A number of learning processes may impinge upon him in this regard, but the most useful type seems to be what will be called here the *experiential* process.

If a pattern of interpersonal behavior has been overlearned to the point that it is experienced as intuitively right, probably the process of learning that will reshape that pattern or replace it with another—which in turn will be experienced as intuitively right—must be very powerful in impact.

At the present state of knowledge about experiential learning some of the most powerful technologies available are those involved in sensitivity training—also called T-groups, or sometimes human resource groups. All of these approaches and their variations are based upon the principles of small-group dynamics. They especially stress the supportive functions of tight group cohesiveness combined with a degree of openness of communication which allows large doses of feedback, both positive and negative, to be exchanged by participants. In such situations previously learned patterns of behavior may be subjected to negative reaction and high levels of dissonance or anxiety aroused. When group cohesiveness is high, however, attempts at new methods of coping are given strong and immediate positive feedback or reinforcement, which tends both to maintain the new behavior and to reduce anxiety.

In effect the participant *experiences* acute sensitivity and awareness of his interpersonal behavior. In the presence of clear and immediate feedback from significant others in the group he begins to learn new behaviors, and as the group communicates approval and acceptance of them he begins to feel the new patterns as intuitively correct and to overlearn them until he is no longer self-conscious about them.

Within this framework the one vital kind of input in a successful counselor education program is an opportunity for experiential learning aimed at changing the immediate-intuitive response mode.

Response Mode B; The Cognitive-Theoretical

A second response mode available to the counselor in preparation can be termed cognitive-theoretical. The student approaches an interpersonal situation in terms of some set of cognitive structures through which he assigns meaning to his perceptions. In early stages of preparation these structures may be naïve and rudimentary. Typically, however, significant inputs in the counselor education program are aimed at upsetting these naïve constructs and replacing them with more psychologically sophisticated ones. This is usually accomplished through a *didactic* program of reading, lecture, and discussion aimed at developing a new theoretical-cognitive framework within which perceptions can be organized and meaning assigned to events.

Again, from what we know about learning it seems plain that the effectiveness of this kind of counselor education input will be determined by the degree of involvement in the process and the clarity of communication which is present. Use of small laboratory and discussion groups, programmed readings, programmed interpersonal relationships, and carefully planned audio-visual materials can probably increase considerably the impact of the didactic aspect of preparation.

Response Mode C; The Empirical-Pragmatic

A third response mode available to counselors in coping with interpersonal tasks can be termed empirical-pragmatic. This mode is based simply on what gives predictable results for the counselor. It involves a set of behaviors which in turn elicit a predictable set of responses from clients. For example, a counselor learns that "when I behave this way clients talk more about their feelings." If counselors in preparation have had almost no experience with the counseling type of interpersonal tasks, they will have a very limited repertory within this mode. As soon as they engage in actual counseling, however, a response repertory will begin to be built. The counselor education input in this mode is the practicum process.

The practicum process represents in many respects a reality testing function. For practicum to be effective, opportunities must be provided for real involvement with clients and for full and open communication between counselors in preparation and clients seeking help. The most important aspect of the practicum process is that feedback to the counselor comes from the client, not merely from fellow students or counselor education staff.

Often so-called practicum treatments are not really practicums at all because the only feedback to the counselor comes from fellow students or faculty. In such situations the treatment is merely a somewhat disguised form of either experiential or didactic work—a modified form of sensitivity training or a didactic instructional session dealing with theoretical constructs used to explain client or counselor behaviors. Such distortions of practicum often result from the limitations built into supervision conducted by tape recordings.

Several methods are available for ensuring that practicum treatments are really that. With one, the unit of practicum is viewed as the case, not the interview. Counselors in preparation should be helped to deal with clients on bases which permit sufficient contact for reasonable goals to be defined and attained so that outcomes can be evaluated.

Another method uses multiple counseling as a form of supervision. That is, two counselors work with a client, both to help the client and to elicit feedback about each other. Still another method uses supervision to stimulate recall or feedback from the client in the presence of the counselor. This method can either involve direct confrontation or be carried out through a medium such as video tape.

The most important characteristic of practicum, in any case, is that the source of behavior-modifying feedback be real clients rather than peers or faculty. We need to prepare counselors who can help clients, not counselors who can merely please supervisors. If a repertory of behaviors in the empirical-pragmatic mode is to be established, the source of reinforcement must be the client.

The Problem of Integration of Response Modes

Three bases for counselor behavior have been discussed and some implications for counselor education relevant to each suggested. Probably the most significant problem in designing learning experiences for counselor education is the integration of these response modes into a natural, comfortable, and effective counseling style for each individual counselor.

Counselor education has generally failed to provide the kind of total educational experience that allows this integration to occur. Instead, counselors in preparation have often been given new theoretical constructs for viewing clients and had suggested to them new behaviors which have not been learned to the point that they are experienced as natural, genuine, or comfortable. They have not been helped to try out the new behaviors in ways which enable them to predict the responses of clients.

The products of this kind of partial and fragmented training are counselors with ambivalent, conflicting, and competing response tendencies. These counselors behave in inconsistent, confused ways, are guilt ridden and ambivalent about their relationships, and are consequently threatened by any attempt to evaluate the results of their efforts.

It is the thesis of this paper that the effective or "fully functioning" counselor is able to integrate the three response modes into one genuine, consistent pattern of behavior which elicits predictable patterns of behavior from clients. Such counselors experience their counseling relationships with greater security and satisfaction, behave with greater consistency, take more risks within the relationship, and are more willing to evaluate the results of counseling.

Toward a Theory of Counselor Education

An examination of the foregoing discussion of counselor education reveals a number of elements which can be combined to form the rudiments of theory of counselor education. Four constructs to conceptualize counselor behaviors which are the output variables in a counselor education process have been described: perceptual sensitivity, cognitive flexibility, consistency of communication, and interpersonal involvement.

Three response modes which form a basis for counselor behavior have been described: the immediate-intuitive, the cognitive-theoretical, and the empirical-pragmatic. Each mode has been linked to a learning process or treatment input method: experiential, didactic, and practical, respectively.

From this theoretical frame of reference it is possible to draw some preliminary hypotheses of a testable nature.

1. In counselor education programs with high loadings of experiential inputs counselors will tend to operate primarily in the immediate-intuitive response mode, with resulting high degrees of perceptual sensitivity and consistency of communication.

2. In counselor education programs with high loadings of didactic input counselors will tend to operate mainly in the theoretical-cognitive response mode, with resulting high degrees of cognitive flexibility.

3. In counselor education programs with high loadings of practicum input counselors will tend to operate in the empirical-pragmatic response mode, experiencing high degrees of inter-personal involvement.

4. In counselor education programs in which high inputs in experiential, didactic, and practical learning processes are main-tained throughout the entire program, counselors will operate in a pattern integrating all three response modes and resulting in high degrees of all four output variables.

Research to test these and other hypotheses drawn from this theory of counselor education is now under way at the University of Minnesota. Instruments have been developed to measure the output variables described here, and learning experiences to maximize inputs on each of the treatment processes are being designed.

Further research will assess the relationships among selection and admission factors, counselor education treatments, counselor behavior outcomes, and various client behavior factors in counseling process and outcome.

Summary

An attempt has been made in this paper to move toward what might be—tentatively at least—termed a theory of counselor education. The position has been taken that it is possible to identify three distinct counseling response modes: immediate-intuitive, cognitive-theoretical, and empirical-pragmatic. Most significant in shaping these modes are three learning processes, termed experiential, didactic, and practical.

It was hypothesized that the crucial challenge facing counselor education is to design sets of learning experiences which will produce an integrated repertory of counselor behaviors that will be simultaneously experienced by the counselor as intuitively right, cognitively correct, and empirically self-validating. It was further suggested that the counselor who functions at this level of integration will be both more effective and more secure.

References

Association for Counselor Education and Supervision Research Committee Report, Minneapolis, Minn., 1967. Mimeographed.

Kell, W., and Mueller, W. *Impact and Change*. New York: Appleton-Century-Crofts, 1967.

Stieper, D., and Wiener, D. *Dimensions of Psychotherapy*. Chicago: Aldine, 1965.

Truax, C., and Carkhuff, R. *Toward Effective Counseling and Psychotherapy*. Chicago: Aldine, 1967.

Counselor Education: A Critical Reaction

CHARLES B. TRUAX
Arkansas Rehabilitation Research and Training Center
University of Arkansas

Reacting critically to Blocher's paper is for me a difficult task. For the most part he has written clearly and cogently, so that I am left with the feeling of being pushed into the role of "devil's advocate."

While it seems true that much of counselor education has involved training (in its narrow sense) rather than education (in its broadest sense), I am personally not at all convinced that social psychology and the psychology of learning have been "the only areas of psychological endeavor to make substantial progress in the past twenty years." One could argue with considerable evidence and cogency that there has been in fact little advance in the psychology of learning. We do have newer sounding terms, so that we now speak of reinforcement (as a bow to Skinner) instead of reward (as Guthrie and people since antiquity have termed it), but it is not at all clear that either kindergartens or university graduate programs have become markedly more effective in promoting learning than their predecessors of twenty, fifty, or five hundred years ago. We have more facts to learn, but there is serious question in my mind that the psychology of learning has given mankind more efficient ways of promoting learning. We might note that most of the current research in learning at the human level is of a rather feebleminded breed that concentrates on rewards of M & M candies, tokens, and other such immature and childish nonsense; it tends to make a game rather than an exciting possibility of the education process.

If the psychology of learning is to be of benefit to mankind in general, I suspect it will become so through the effort of such tangential fields as counseling, which, as Blocher says, "has finally begun to address itself to the task of harnessing and *humanizing* it" (my italics).

I could not agree more closely with Blocher when he speaks of involvement, communication, perceptual sensitivity, authenticity, openness, and confrontiveness. Whether we call these accurate empathy, nonpossessive warmth, and genuineness or refer to them in terms of cognitive flexibility, interpersonal involvement, or whatnot, we are speaking of very human qualities that have much more profoundly affected my own life and the lives of those whom I have come to know than would all the M & M candies and plastic tokens this world can ever produce.

While I agree with Blocher's views that counselors in preparation are essentially people attempting to learn more effective interpersonal relationships, which in turn will allow them to facilitate the learning of others, surely counselors must also have a fund of *expert* knowledge that is quite separate from their interpersonal skills; if they are to be of any value in vocational guidance, they must know the facts about job markets, requisite skills and rewards, differential salaries in different industries where the same skills are employed, the requirements for training, aptitude, interest, and a host of other relevant facts.

Similarly, they must of course have a wide range of expert knowledge including the factors associated with learning achievement, marital relationships, parent-child relationships, community resources and community relationships, as well as a broad understanding of human nature, values, and the recurrent predicaments of human existence.

At the heart of Dr. Blocher's viewpoint are three abstracted theoretical concepts presumably dealing with differential aspects of counseling behavior: the immediate-intuitive aspect, the cognitive-theoretical aspect, and the empirical-practical aspect. Although it may be helpful to differentiate them for theoretical analysis, the counselor himself probably includes all three aspects in any given response that he makes to a client; or it may even be that these three theoretically specified response modes do not correspond to reality. There is some evidence (such as Wrenn, 1960) to suggest that little correspondence exists between one's theoretic-intellectual view of counseling and the actual responses made to clients.

We might suspect that counseling, like all learned human behavior, is role specific (elicited under one stimulus complex but not under another) so that intellectual-theoretic learning in the classroom from the faculty is acquired in relation to the stimulus complex of academicia and so is not role specific to the actual practice of a counselor.

There is also abundant evidence (especially Renneker, 1967) suggesting that both beginning and experienced counselors and therapists are relatively impervious to client or patient feedback. Thus, it is clear that counselors and therapists by and large hear only what they want to hear from their clients and at times wind up discussing at length what turns out to be their distorted memories rather than what the client originally actually said.

In short, it could be argued that actual counselor behavior operates mainly if not exclusively at the "immediate-intuitive" level. This is the level where responses come from overlearned past habits of interpersonal relating: the counselor is doing what *"feels natural"* or "feels right." It could be argued that responses at the immediate-intuitive level (overlearned habits) can be changed not only through peer and group influences but also through the broader range of didactic and experiential learnings that can be specified in terms of current learning nomenclature.

While it is possible that sensitivity training or T-group train-ing can produce changes in experiential learning, *this has yet to be adequately demonstrated.* I cannot share Blocher's unre-served endorsement of the usual sensitivity training approach. Those who advocate sensitivity training have been almost uniquely unconcerned with evaluation of results. We do not have adequate research showing what kinds of sensitivity train-ing lead to what kinds of behavior changes in the trainees. More-over, it seems likely that with the diversity of psychological con-ditions occurring in sensitivity training groups it is a "for better or for worse" phenomenon leading in some cases to positive changes and in others to negative or deteriorative changes. If sensitivity training can be useful, it should be more clearly spec-ified both in terms of the characteristics and conditions in-volved and in terms of the predicted consequent behavior changes in its participants.

Since the training of counselors involves many of the same types of behavior changes that effective counseling should pro-duce (especially those at the immediate-intuitive level), we must ask why counselor educators so frequently use radically different educational procedures in training a counselor from those they recommend for changing a client.

A massive amount of evidence, involving well over a hundred research studies, now indicates that the interpersonal qualities or skills described by Blocher and defined under the general terms "accurate empathic understanding," "nonpossessive warmth," and "genuineness" are central to a wide variety of therapeutically induced behavior changes in clients—whether these clients are hospitalized psychotics, juvenile delinquents, college under-achievers, fourth-grade students in arithmetic or reading, out-patient neurotics, physically and emotionally handicapped vo-cational rehabilitation clients, or general run-of-the-mill counsel-ing center clients (Truax and Carkhuff, 1967). There is also considerable evidence that in less than one hundred hours of training both lay personnel and beginning counseling trainees can be brought to significantly higher levels of these interper-sonal skills. The program of training specifically involves (1) the didactic reinforcing and shaping procedure based on peer pressure and peer ratings, using research scales measuring these interpersonal qualities to provide feedback of the beginning counselor's actual functioning with clients; (2) a quasi group therapy experience that facilitates the trainee's self-exploration and integration of theoretic, experiential, and didactic learnings; and (3) the offering of relatively high levels of empathy, warmth, and genuineness by the supervisors, both in classroom and in quasi group therapy and supervisory contexts.

Identifying Therapeutic Skills

These therapeutic skills of empathy, warmth, and genuineness would seem central to the counselor educator's own effectiveness in inducing changes in the student trainee. While certain knowledge of counselor educators' mode of operation in producing desired behavior changes in trainees must await further research, some tentative explication can now be made.

1. The supervisor's offering of accurate empathic understanding, nonpossessive warmth, and genuineness to the trainee provide a safe or nonthreatening relationship which minimizes or reduces the presence of threat, which in turn minimizes the trainee's defensiveness and inhibition. Experimental evidence is abundantly available to indicate that threat increases anxiety, which in turn interferes with complex learning.

2. The offering of these high levels of conditions, through the principle of reciprocal affect, induces positive feelings on the part of the trainee, which co-vary with the warmth, etc., offered by the supervisor. From recent evidence (Bandura and Perloff, 1967) it is clear that a person's self-reinforcement system is at least as effective as an externally imposed reinforcement system. The crucial importance of the patient's self-concept system lies in its control of his self-reinforcement system, which in turn markedly affects his behavior (as suggested by Marston, 1965). The presence of favorable conditions tends to elicit and reinforce self-concepts and also to foster positive expectations or induce hopes, which, as expectancy studies and placebo studies have shown, significantly influence a person's behavioral functioning.

3. As recent research has shown, accurate empathic responses involve a high degree of implicit and explicit confrontation

(Berenson and Mitchell, 1967). This, and the verbalization of the fact that the person is not functioning maximally, demands a commitment for change from the trainee.

4. The interpersonal skills of empathy, warmth, and genuineness have powerful reward value or reinforcing properties (Truax, 1966, 1967) and can therefore be used selectively in the specific shaping of the trainee's behavior.

5. The offering of propitious conditions provides a model of an effective therapist in the form of the supervisor, which, according to evidence on modeling and imitation learning (Bandura and Walters, 1965), will induce behavior change.

6. Warmth, as Shoben (1948, 1949) and others have noted, has potent counterconditioning value in the extinguishing of a person's fear and learned avoidance and defensive reactions in human interpersonal relating. Particularly, nonpossessive warmth, through the principle of reciprocal affect, tends automatically to elicit warmth and comfort responses in the trainee: responses incompatible with an anxiety or a defensive response. As the trainee becomes conditioned to the new response of elicited warmth, it competes with anxiety, avoidance, or defensiveness cues associated with interpersonal relating.

7. The high levels of therapeutic conditions and accurate empathy in particular lead to cognitive changes via the trainee's self-labeling or insight into "what leads to what." Self-labeling, either by the trainee or by the supervisor, as Mowrer (1939), Dollard and Miller (1950), and Farber (1963) have noted, facilitates both generalization and discrimination learning. Thus, empathic responses facilitate awareness of response-reinforcement contingencies and thereby influence the trainee's overt performance. The research of Dulaney (1961), Erickson (1962), and Farber (1963) strongly indicates that empathic responses promoting recognition of response-reinforcement contingencies are effective in producing desired behavior changes.

8. Low ratings by peers of the trainee's attempts to provide warmth, etc., provide avoidance conditioning training that in-

hibits in the trainee any overlearned, unempathic, cold, rejecting, and "professional role" responses.

9. Studies in mass communication, opinion change, and persuasion, both in small-group processes, in police confessions, and
in mass public opinion change, indicate that the higher the level
of personal involvement between communicator and recipient,
the higher the degree of group cohesiveness (the warmer and
more empathic the communication), the greater the opinion
change or persuasion in the recipient (Zimbardo, 1960; Winthrop, 1958; Berkowitz, 1954; van Zelst, 1951; Schachter, 1951;
and French and Snyder, 1959).

The Search for Specific Elements in Counselor Education

In concluding, I would like to argue for more specific identification of the elements of counselor education, since it seems
likely that counselor education, like the counseling process itself, can lead on the one hand to positive trainee changes or on
the other to deteriorative trainee behavior changes, *depending
upon the actual psychological conditions provided during training.* Thus, some kinds of didactic training probably result in cognitive flexibility and others in inflexibility. Some kinds of experiential training lead to perceptual sensitivity and consistency
of communcation while others result in perceptual insensitivity
and inconsistency of communication. Some kinds of practicum
training lead to personal involvement while others lead to avoidance of intense interpersonal relationships. The more general
the theory, the more likely that a variety of educators will agree
with it but the more useless it will be in practice; the more specific the theory, the more disagreement it will arouse among
educators but the more useful it will be in practice—and the
greater the possibility that research based on it will produce
new knowledge.

It is time we took counselor education seriously, for it is central to effective or ineffective counseling practices. It is more
than sobering to note that no good evidence exists to suggest
that the counselors we are producing today are in any way more
effective than those produced ten, twenty, or even more years

ago; indeed, the average counselor of twenty years ago and the average counselor of today may achieve no results beyond those seen in a no-treatment control group. At the very least, we must begin to carefully evaluate *effects of student trainees on clients during training: we must begin to weed out those who have no effect or deteriorative effect on clients and reward those producing positive changes in their clients.*

References

Bandura, A., and Perloff, B.   Relative efficacy of self-monitored and externally-imposed reinforcement systems. *Journal of Personality and Social Psychology*, 1967, 7, 111–116.

Bandura, A., and Walters, R. H.   *Social Learning and Personality Development.* New York: Holt, Rinehart & Winston, 1965.

Berenson, B. G., and Mitchell, K. M.   Level of therapist functioning, frequency and type of confrontation. Unpublished manuscript, Arkansas Rehabilitation Research and Training Center, University of Arkansas, 1967.

Berkowitz, L.   Group standards, cohesiveness, and productivity. *Human Relations*, 1954, 7, 509–519.

Dollard, J., and Miller, N. E.   *Personality and Psychotherapy.* New York: McGraw-Hill, 1950.

Dulaney, D. E.   Hypotheses and habits in verbal "operant conditioning." *Journal of Abnormal Social Psychology*, 1961, 63, 251–263.

Erickson, D. W. (ed.).   *Behavior and Awareness: A Symposium of Research and Interpretation.* Durham, N.C.: Duke University Press, 1962.

Farber, I. E.   The things people say to themselves. *American Psychologist*, 1963, 18, 185–197.

French, J. R. P., and Snyder, R.   Leadership in interpersonal power. In D. Cartwright (ed.), *Studies in Social Power.* Ann Arbor: University of Michigan Press, 1959.

Marston, A. R.   Imitation, self-reinforcement, and reinforcement of another person. *Journal of Personality and Social Psychology*, 1965, 2, 255–261.

Mowrer, O. H.   A stimulus-response analysis of anxiety and its role as a reinforcing agent. *Psychological Review*, 1939, *46*, 553–565.

Renneker, R.   Recorded psychotherapy: Antidote to faulty memory. In *Six Views of Psychotherapy: Alternatives to Classical Psychoanalysis*. International Science Press, Inc. 1967.

Schachter, S.   Deviation, rejection and communication. *Journal of Abnormal Social Psychology*, 1951, *46*, 190–207.

Shoben, E. J.   A learning theory interpretation of psychotherapy. *Harvard Educational Review*, 1948, *18*, 129–145.

Shoben, E. J.   Psychotherapy as a problem in learning theory. *Psychological Bulletin*, 1949, *46*, 366–392.

Truax, C. B.   Some implications of behavior therapy for psychotherapy. *Journal of Counseling Psychology*, 1965, *13*, 160–170.

Truax, C. B.   Therapist reinforcement of patient self-exploration and therapeutic outcome in group psychotherapy. Unpublished manuscript, Arkansas Rehabilitation Research and Training Center, University of Arkansas, 1967.

Truax, C. B., and Carkhuff, R. R.   *Toward Effective Counseling and Psychotherapy: Training and Practice*. Chicago: Aldine, 1967.

van Zelst, R. H.   Worker popularity and job satisfaction. *Personnel Psychology*, 1951, *4*, 405–412.

Winthrop, H.   Relations between appeal value and highbrow status on some radio and television programs. *Psychological Reports*, 1958, *4*, 53–54.

Wrenn, R. L.   Counselor orientation: Theoretical or situational? *Journal of Counseling Psychology*, 1960, *7*, 40–45.

Zimbardo, P. G.   Involvement and communication discrepancy as determinants of opinion conformity. *Journal of Abnormal Social Psychology*, 1950, *60*, 86–94.

The Encounter

The primary focus of this discussion, unlike the others, was upon counselor education rather than counseling. General agreement was expressed that there is need for "hard data" regarding the effectiveness of our programs. This can be judged only by actual behavior changes in the counselors themselves as assessed by their ability to facilitate change in clients. The difficulties of obtaining such data were raised, but the participants in the discussion insisted that the need is for carefully designed programs calculated to produce specific changes in counselors, with adequate evaluative procedures to ensure that the changes take place.

BLOCHER: I don't really think counselor education is doing a very good job of preparing counselors. What we have done for the past fifteen or twenty years is teach doctoral students a lot about counseling and we have not changed their behavior as counselors. We have given master's students a lot of conflicting, confusing, disorganizing bits and pieces of information. Then we have given them a practicum in which they have tried, in a very short period of time, with people who were not really clients, to put all of this back together again. In fact, what has happened is that they have been very insecure and very guilt-ridden about their inadequacies. They have searched for the things they can do to avoid doing any actual counseling when they get out in the schools. This is probably good both for them and for their potential clients in many cases.

We do have the knowledge to prepare much better counselors than we are preparing now. The job is to try to design some learning treatments which will have an impact on the counseling behavior of students in our programs. We ought to start evaluating the effects of our programs on the counseling behavior of people.

TRUAX: I am pretty well convinced that most of the persons here have not done any systematic evaluation of their own training efforts either in terms of the counseling behavior of their students or in terms of the clients these counselors will be seeing. If I talk to friends in the business world, they suggest that we are pretty naïve. Any company of any size that has any product does have some quality control studies going on all the time. Only a small handful of studies have attempted to look at what effect a counselor trainee is having on clients. Scarcely ever, in any of the helping professions, does a supervisor look at the effect his trainee is having on his client. He is apparently more interested in whether the trainee is talking a good line.

I wonder how many of you would be willing to go back and make some strong effort to look at the client. At most we have practicum students play tapes and talk about their tapes. I have known therapists who do things quite differently from the way I do and they get results. If I only listened to their tapes, I might conclude that something that was effective was ineffective and vice versa. We should go back and see what effect we are having on clients.

The kind of person who will communicate warmth to a supervisor may not communicate it to a peer or may not communicate it to a client. Another person who is very cold and perhaps hostile toward authority figures and supervisors may be extremely warm with a client.

BLOCHER: It might be much more important for a student to be successful in helping one obese client lose weight or one client quit smoking or one client pass a language exam than it would to play ten tapes of the first thirty minutes of an interview with a client who was recruited to come over to help with the practicum.

GIBB: You think, then, Dr. Truax, that it is very important for people in training to get some clear indication of how they are perceived by the client—so they can get direct feedback on their behavior in order to change their behavior to get better therapeutic outcomes?

TRUAX: Right, more than just perceptions. I am not convinced by the kind of direct feedback we get from a client in an interview. I think we ought to take it a step farther and say, for example, "Is the person getting better grades?" If not, if he just reports feeling better but not getting better grades (if that is his problem), we should know it. It is quite possible that a person could be warm, empathic, and genuine and still not be having an effective impact.

LEVY: I don't think we know enough yet to know what kinds of changes we can expect from what kinds of clients to judge the effectiveness or quality of the student trainee from his effect upon a particular client. It might be grossly unfair.

TRUAX: I couldn't disagree with that more. I don't really see a major measurement problem. As a therapist, I'm not interested in a one percent change. I darn well wouldn't spend my time, energy, or anything else if I didn't feel the changes I can produce are obvious, and not subtle, mystical, unobservable things. I think it is almost fraudulent the way the ABEPP exams are set up on the basis of talking a good line rather than the ability to effect desirable changes. We have the audacity to sit back and say that we can evaluate one's intellectual knowledge, one's educational level, with a pretty small sample and we feel comfortable with it in giving or not giving degrees. It would be no more difficult to look at the effects counselors have on clients. It would be just as easy to pick four or five clients, do a standard pre- and post-evaluation, and base the exam on that.

An exchange followed regarding the degree to which existing evidence would allow accurate estimation of the amount of change that could be reasonably expected. No consensus was reached on how possible this was. There was some agreement, however, that counselor education needs to move to the point at which a trainee's competence is judged on the basis of behavior change in clients rather than on his modeling particular behaviors regarded as theoretically appropriate. Truax suggested that formal courses, as such, be done away with and the emphasis be put on reading lists, peer group discussions, periodic examinations, vicarious experiences through literature and other media, and closely supervised counseling experience designed to increase effectiveness.

This led the group into a general discussion of the effectiveness of video tape in furnishing feedback. Several persons had attended a counselor educators' seminar at Michigan State University where video tape had been used to furnish feedback to the supervisors as well as to students and clients. They were impressed with the amount of observable change in a relatively short time. One participant estimated that the amount of change normally produced in a semester could be produced in half that time. Dr. Gibb reviewed some of his experiences with video tape in small-group work with the conviction that it held high promise for developing effective nonverbal behavior in a very short time. No one related negative experiences with video tape. Dr. Pepinsky did, however, point out that video tape, like so many other fads in psychology, needed to be questioned—that perhaps we might properly be cautious about its use.

At several points throughout the seminar Dr. Pepinsky had suggested that there might be prior questions about what counseling was for, which should be discussed before methods of counseling or counselor preparation were taken up. He began to raise some of these questions here again, thus initiating what became perhaps the most heated discussion in the seminar, in part because many participants had difficulty understanding the meaning of Dr. Pepinsky's concerns and in part because he was asking searching questions about the entire enterprise of counseling. Dr. Truax responded first to Dr. Pepinsky's question.

TRUAX: I am personally, by nature, a skeptic. Yet on the other hand I have to teach something because I accepted the job of doing it. What I can do is look over the research findings, the evidence, and try to produce new evidence as well, and from that say that the most likely conclusion is that if you know this and act these ways you will be more effective than if you don't. If I can't come to that point, then I shouldn't really be teaching anything at all.

PEPINSKY: To me the alternative has suggested itself. There are times when one is desperately tempted to fill a void, when in fact there is a constructive alternative open to him.

TRUAX: There is a great deal of evidence, a massive amount of evidence, to suggest that certain kinds of procedures (empathy, warmth, genuineness, for example) are more effective than nothing or other kinds of approaches. I think I have an obligation to teach that to any prospective trainee, while on reading lists and tests I force people to read theories which I frankly believe are nonsense. But I require that they know them, just on the principle that they should be knowledgeable. I don't think it is a responsible stance for an educator to say, "If this is a fairy tale, the best procedure is to know twenty fairy tales." Even if one were to agree that that is what they are.

GIBB: I think you can dodge the fairy tale issue by looking at outcomes. There would be some agreement that the effectiveness of the counselor depends upon his behavior in the situation. So if we focus a training program directly on the behavior of the counselor and some way of upgrading it so that it becomes a continual doing and upgrading of the doing—there is ample evidence that his doing can change—he can become more effective.

PEPINSKY: Have you men who keep talking about evidence ever been cross-examined about it by a lawyer? This is a very interesting experience, and lawyers don't believe the evidence.

GIBB: Yes. I have been in some very grilling situations. I think there *is* good evidence. I was looking last night at the material you have in your recent book and it comports with a summary Lorraine and I were making of similar kinds of evidence that I think are even stronger than those that you cite. There are a lot of things we *do* know about behavior in a therapy situation.

PEPINSKY: I find it very important to understand what you are saying as a matter of "In whose view is this being said? In whose view is this convincing? For what reason does it become convincing?" I don't mean this to be mischievous.

GIBB: But what are you saying about what we are saying? Are you saying you don't believe that there are some behaviors that can be changed? What is your position on that? Can behavior be changed or not?

PEPINSKY: That's like "Have you stopped beating your wife?" (*laughter*) I'm saying that it might be a matter of what it is that we are treating as behavior, what it is that we consider as evidence of a change.

LEVY: I think, Dr. Pepinsky, that part of the reason you are confusing people is that it is out of context. People here are concerned with counseling theory and counselor education. I think what you are saying would be better received in a seminar concerned with the sociology of knowledge.

PEPINSKY: My God! Why is that so irrelevant to what a counselor educator is up to?

BLOCHER: I can appreciate your view, but as a counselor educator, when I go back next week, I've got to do the things that seem best to me in terms of the knowledge I have. I think it would be a tremendous help then to have you look at me and what I do and raise these questions with me. We have a proposal now for a social psychologist on our staff to ask just these questions—to stand back and look at us, what we believe, what our fairy tales are and what effects they have on our counselors. Then we must look at what effects those counselors have on their clients when they go out into the school taking the fairy tales with them.

I believe this is a most helpful thing to do, but in the meantime I still have to do what I think is best in terms of the knowledge I have. One of the things we haven't done in counselor education is to have others ask these questions. We *have* insulated ourselves from the views of people outside and have taken a very narrow view of what we do.

PEPINSKY: Obviously I have my biases. I would want you to examine my ritual in the same way, open it to the same kind of scrutiny. Furthermore, there are things I have to take on faith in my own searching activities. Yet I take the same attitude toward my own searching activity. I have the same impressions about a lot of the technologists who are grinding out science with a desperate conviction that doing something is a constructive alternative. I live in a country that is getting flooded with outputs of this kind. I'm not being mischievous. If I'm out of context, then I have to ask, "Leon, where does this alien go to register?"

BLOCHER: I think, practically, one of the stupid things we have done in counselor education is to set up standards ourselves and then ask our buddies over in the next institution to look at us and tell us how well we are doing. What we ought to be doing is to get people from as far away as possible who will raise as many of these nasty, ugly questions as they can and force us to look at them. I think this is essential to the health of our enterprise.

PEPINSKY: I do raise these out of the honest conviction that it would be catastrophic not to. They do make us uncomfortable, but I think they are essential.

BLOCHER: They ought to make us uncomfortable, but not so uncomfortable that they immobilize us. We've got to look at ourselves, but we can't stop the enterprise in the meantime.

Epilogue

So the seminar ended, on a note of urgency for action in the midst of an inadequate body of knowledge. In one sense, the irony of Pepinsky's questions is that the urgency for action has been precipitated by a society that not only has been willing to buy the professional services offered by counselors but has in fact legislated the purchase of services which the profession is not yet prepared to offer. The crises that precipitated short-term crash programs (e.g., Project Cause) intended to prepare counselors and para-professionals long before the profession had done its homework, and the request for services in the Job Corps and other programs of the Office of Economic Opportunity has created a flurry of activity to strengthen the counselor's knowledge of and adequacy with the deprived. Our society's felt needs immediately after Sputnik resulted in the NDEA Counseling and Guidance Institutes intended to prepare counselors to identify and work with the gifted. The focus of the institutes has tended to change as the country's needs were identified—not by counselors but largely by politicians.

Counselor educators have responded as quickly and often as thoughtlessly as automatons, believing that because society asked for their services they could, indeed, meet the need. We have not been willing to consider the "constructive alternatives." We have not been "actors" nearly as much as we have been "reactors." We have not been willing or able to specify what we *can* do with any great detail in order to direct the larger society in its use of our specialty.

Blocher and Truax emphasized how critical it is to determine a counselor's effectiveness by the change produced in clients rather than his ability to recapitulate theories or please supervisors. Even though Bordin stressed the need for solid theoretical grounding, he and Vance seemed to agree that the real proof is in the ability of the counselor to effect the change desired. Gibb, who appeared to deny the intent to change a client's behavior, has at the basis of his theory an expectation that his "desirelessness of change" will bring about well-defined and conceptualized changes. He, too, would "certify" only those counselors who were "*effective*." Patterson insisted that with his system counselors would be better prepared as therapists than most graduates of four-year clinical programs. With all the emphasis on "effectiveness" there was little consideration of the relation of the changes produced by counselors to the needs of society.

In the larger sense, then, Pepinsky has asked the most significant question: "What is the social meaning of our profession—or does it have any?" Questions of counseling effectiveness and subsequent questions of the effectiveness of our preparation programs most often begin where that question ends, taking it and a good deal else for granted. Psychologists are rarely good philosophers. Further, counselors are compassionate persons disposed to act in relief of misery and ask questions later. In a world of pain, "later" rarely comes. The need for action must be tempered by the needs for direction and for research. They are inseparable. We must act, but we must ask the hard questions too. This is what Dr. Levy was attempting to help us see in his discussion of paradox and the need to *act* in the face of inconsistency. It is true of us as well as of our clients.

Index

8 3 3